IDENTITY CRISIS

FRANK SANTORA

ISBN: 978-0-9793192-5-9

Published by

LIFEBRIDGE
BOOKS
P.O. BOX 49428
CHARLOTTE, NC 28277

Printed in the United States of America.

ACKNOWLEDGMENTS

Nobel Peace Prize recipient Elie Wiesel once observed, "There is divine beauty in learning, just as there is human beauty in tolerance. To learn means to accept the postulate that life did not begin at my birth. Others have been here before me, and I walk in their footsteps. The books I have read were composed by generations of fathers and sons, mothers and daughters, teachers and disciples. I am the sum total of their experiences, their quests. And so are you."

In writing this book, perhaps more than at any other time, I have understood this truth. And it is with this in mind that I want to express my gratitude to the following:

My wife Lisa, who is my best friend and life partner, and our children, Nicole and Joseph, for their unconditional love, trust, support, and inspiration.

My parents, Frank and Fran, for teaching me by example the true nature of our heavenly Father.

My spiritual leaders, Dad Fletcher, Rick Renner, and Anthony Storino, for their never-ending lessons in both practical and spiritual truth.

The people of Faith Ministries, who honor me with the privilege of leading them daily.

And of course my editor, Dr. Courtenay Caublé, who has brought out the best in me and without whom this book would never have been. He has become a treasured friend.

3

CONTENTS

FOREWORD

When my friend Frank Santora asked me to write a foreword for his book *Identity Crisis*, I gladly agreed to do so, not realizing how significant and timely the book would prove to be in my own life. But as soon as I started reading, I realized that Frank's book was like a message sent from heaven to meet the exact need I was facing at that very moment.

God has enabled me, along with my wife Denise and our team, to do many "big" things that others thought were impossible. Out of these experiences I have written my own books about overcoming insurmountable challenges and accomplishing what looks impossible on the surface. But at the time Frank's book came to me for review, I was facing one of the most challenging opportunities of my life; and even though I had experienced many victories in the past, I was still lying awake at night, asking myself, *Are we really able to do this?*

Then I started reading this book; and if I had never progressed any farther than Chapter One, the positive effect on my state of mind would have been enormous! It encouraged me to make the decision to step forward by faith so that I could tackle and win the greatest faith challenge I had ever faced!

There are numerous books on the market about leadership, developing your potential, and cultivating the gifts and talents hidden in your life. But the book you hold in your hands right now is unique among these. Such publications often contain only rehashed information that authors have pulled from other sources. In contrast, *Identity Crisis* provides a perspective on those themes that is as fresh as a breeze from heaven blowing over you to refresh, encourage, and challenge you. And I guarantee that by the time you have finished reading, you *will* be inspired to break free from whatever aspect of grasshopper mentality might be standing in your way!

I encourage you not to let this book sit untouched and unread on your bookshelf. Get the maximum benefit that God wants you to receive from the message contained within these pages. Open up this book and immediately start to devour it. *You'll never regret that you did!*

− Rick Renner
Best-selling author, pastor, conference speaker, and television producer

PREFACE

Y ou may have seen the television commercial showing two elderly women sitting on a couch, gloating over their new lives, and speaking with men's voices.

No, they haven't had sex change operations. It's a commercial alerting watchers to the hazards of identity theft. Anyone who has ever been victimized by this criminal act knows its effects can be devastating.

But I believe that our world is besieged by a much more destructive catastrophe—by what I see as an Identity Crisis which threatens each of us if we aren't prepared to guard ourselves against it. Low individual self-esteem can arguably be seen as the cause of personal and social problems including depression, abusiveness, broken marriages, suicide, and racial injustice.

Success in life and consequent happiness largely depend on the sort of personal orientation that comes from knowing where we came from, why we are here, and where we are going.

Unfortunately, society does little to help us discover our significance, but rather reinforces our Identity Crisis by conditioning us to focus on our shortcomings instead of on our unique personal strengths. Think back to your schooldays, for instance, when your teacher put an X next to each of your wrong answers on a test instead of encouraging check marks next to the answers you got right.

This is just one example, but it illustrates my point—that since childhood, we have been encouraged (or discouraged might be a better word) to focus on what is wrong about ourselves instead of on what is right. And this negative emphasis has contributed to causing generations of people to see themselves as inferior, infecting them with what I call "grasshopper mentality."

Although luck, upbringing, schooling, and being in the right place at the right time can play a part in our personal success or failure, what matters most is how we see ourselves.

I believe the solution to the Identity Crisis plague is for each of us to seek to see ourselves *as God sees us* instead of allowing ourselves to be turned aside by the judgments of others or discouraged or blocked by passing circumstances. I know that many have been conditioned to believe God judges us by our imperfections and mistakes; but this is far from the truth. God sees each of us as a More Than Conqueror who is limitless in his or her God-given potential.

I have written this book to help you see yourself in a new and more productive way—one that will help you find your true identity. I believe that once you are able to view yourself through God's eyes, your outlook will brighten and your life will begin to move in a divinely intended direction.

– Frank Santora

CHAPTER ONE

SEEING YOURSELF AS GOD SEES YOU

*Mikhael, who for too long saw
himself as a grasshopper instead of, as
his name proclaims, like God.*

I am the last of a foolish people, and yet you sit at my feet, Beriah, grandson of my son, expecting wisdom. Perhaps the last breaths of a dying fool can offer such. If you must listen, may it please the Lord that wisdom is what you hear.

Is the tent flap open? I am cold. Pull up the sheepskin across my chest.

That is better. Blessings upon you, Beriah.

I do not know why I am the last. Perhaps because I saw him first. I was a boy in Egypt, sent to carry straw by my father. I had to carry twice as much that day, for the overseer had beaten my older brother Enan so much he could not walk. My eyes were filled with tears for his pain, and even as I carried the straw, my arms shook with fear that the overseer might turn his wrath on me as he had on Enan.

My grandmother had told me of the Deliverer. She said the Lord would send him and he would come to take us all back to the lands of Abraham, Isaac, and Jacob. She told us the stories at night, when the Egyptians could no longer make us work and our bones ached so that all we could do was lie beside the fire

11

and listen. She told us of Abraham's wealth and of the Land that he had been promised and of beautiful Sara, who laughed, yet bore a son when she was as old as I am now. Also of Isaac and Rebecca, of Jacob and Leah, mother of our tribe, and of Rachel and the beloved sons. I learned of Joseph and how his words had become as the laws of the Pharaoh himself, and of how he brought his father and brothers to Egypt to save them from famine. And always, always, she told of the Lord and said He would be faithful to us and send a Deliverer.

But my father scoffed and said the Lord must have stayed behind in Canaan. And Enan observed that if Joseph had been the reason we were in Egypt, then Joseph was a fool and not a hero.

If I speak ill of my ancestors, may the Lord forgive me. But my father's sin has followed me too long, and I would turn it away from you, Beriah.

The wind blows through the tent flap. Can you knot it closed?

The wind was hot that day. I came upon a high pile of stones, the start of a wall, unfinished and abandoned. They made a place of shadow, so I rested for a moment inside the shade, pressing my bare back against the stones to take their coolness into me. I had intended to stop for just a moment, but I was weary, and the sun was burning and the stones were cool, and I fell asleep.

The shouts of the overseer woke me. I was immediately afraid; I knew if he saw me sleeping there, he would beat me with his rod. Already I could hear heavy blows and the cries of another slave. I peered through a crack in the rocks and saw the overseer striking a youth from Ishvi's clan. I closed my eyes in fear and prayed that the Deliverer would come. I did not know what else to do. I feared to move, I feared to speak up, I even feared to stay where I was. I heard stone scrape on stone and knew someone had grabbed a rock from my wall. I looked up in terror, certain the overseer had discovered me, but there was no one there. I heard a young man's voice cry out —not the cry of a slave, but the shout of a person used to being obeyed.

I looked back through the crack and saw a man dressed in the white robes of a prince, though I could see he was not Egyptian. He held the stone from my wall high in his hands, and he brought it down on the overseer's head. I saw the overseer fall, and there was blood on the stone and on the prince's hands, and I hid my face behind my hands and was certain he would kill me next.

But he didn't. When I found the courage to look again, the prince was gone, and so was the overseer's body.

❖

The only person left was the youth, who lay with his head on a bundle of white linen, senseless but alive. I was certain the Deliverer had come.

But when I told my father that night, he became angry. "That is no Deliverer! He is the false princeling Moses, who lives in the Pharaoh's house and eats his meat while the rest of his brethren dine on scraps! Would that he had thrown the stone on himself, for all the good it will do us! Now Pharaoh will send a new overseer, worse than the first. And he will blame us for the death when it becomes known!"

The next morning my father demanded Ishvi's clan turn the linen over to Pharaoh as proof of our innocence. He fought with the youth's father, who wanted to keep the linen; and when they were fighting, Moses himself rode upon a chariot and commanded them to stop. But my father defied him, telling Moses that he knew about the murder. Then I saw fear on the prince's face, and Moses fled. For the first time I doubted the Deliverer would ever come.

---❖---

*I am thirsty, Beriah. Bring me but a sip of
goat's milk; I can hold no more upon my tongue.*

My father's predictions came true. Even though Pharaoh knew Moses had slain the overseer, the new replacement was worse than the first. He always traveled with two guards; and when he was finished beating a slave, the guards would add their blows as well. Enan died under their rods, as did our father, and I was left to lead our tiny house. Grandmother still told her stories, but not as surely as before; and when she died, no one repeated them anymore.

And then, when I had all but forgotten that day among the stones, Moses returned. He was no longer the proud young prince dressed in white linens and gold collar. He was an old man in dusty shepherd's robes, leaning on a thick, twisted staff. But he was Moses; and if his voice no longer sounded as if he expected to be obeyed, it sounded more as if he should. And this time he promised deliverance, and promised it from the Lord.

We did not know what to believe. Some were eager to follow him, but others said doing so would just bring more sorrow on us all. I remembered my father's predictions after the overseer's murder, and I agreed with them, though my voice carried no more weight at that time than it does now. Mikhael BarAnath is a name of no report among the people.

At first it seemed we were correct. Moses had no more appeared before his foster brother, the Pharaoh, than new commands came down: we were to gather our own straw for the bricks. No longer would Pharaoh supply it. We complained to Moses, but he only assured us this was the Lord's plan.

And then came the plagues; I do not need to tell of them again, for you have heard about them all your life and can name each yourself— blood, frogs, gnats, disease, flies, boils, hail, locusts, darkness, and death. The Lord proved His power, to Pharaoh and all of Egypt.

But of all who believed it true, we for whom it was done believed it least of all. A multitude of fools we were. The Lord parted the sea and drowned Pharaoh's chariots, and still we grumbled. He fed us with manna and quail and water drawn from bare rock, and still we whined. He led us with cloud and fire, and still we danced before a crudely molded idol and called that misshapen calf a god. And when He turned His wrath on us with serpents and plagues and fire, we cowered in fear, believing only because we were afraid not to.

We were faithless fools!

Yet the Lord and Moses led us on. They did not forsake us, though we deserved to be abandoned. And when finally we arrived at the Promised Land, the gift of God to Abraham, Isaac, Jacob, and all their sons, it seemed that we at last had the opportunity to share their faith. How could we not? The Promise lay before us, gleaming green beyond the desert.

On that day, Moses summoned the leaders of the tribes and asked them to select twelve young men, brave and cunning, who would go into the land of the Canaanites and observe and bring back a report about its riches and its people.

How much pride I had when Pagiel chose my own son, Sethur, to represent the tribe of Asher! This was the very day you were born and Sethur named you Beriah in honor of the father of our clan, because we knew then the clan and our tribe would look to our house as leaders! And indeed, for the next month people came to me for advice, eager to hear the words of Mikhael, father of Sethur, to learn what wisdom had enabled me to rear such a son. How much folly I breathed then, I do not know, but it was all folly.

I heard the sound of hammers on stones outside—the men grinding their swords sharp and honing spearheads, each more deadly than a serpent's sting. In those days, the sounds echoed through the camp. And why should they not? We had defeated the Amalekites, and we were no longer a rabble of slaves, but an army in our own right. Men boasted we could now face the Pharaoh himself, forgetting that only two years earlier we had trembled in fear at the distant whisper of his chariots. Now we were arming for the land of Canaan, certain the people there would be no match for us. Forty days we honed our blades, until Sethur and the other eleven returned.

Oh, the wonder of the land of which Joshua and Caleb spoke! I saw the grapes, thick as eggs, trailing in a single cluster as long as the height of a man! I myself tasted honey from Sethur's own pouch, sweeter than any in all of Egypt. They told us of water flowing freely, springs and wells throughout the land, of a mighty highland lake to the north, of the mighty Jordan flowing through rich fields and forest—a land where a man could have a home of stone and wood instead of goat hair, where he could till the soil and have his food outside his door instead of having to wander through sand and rock, scraping for whatever might be found.

Then Sethur shook his head. To my shame forever, it was Sethur who first spoke faithlessly against Joshua and Caleb's encouraging report. "But," he said, that faithless word, "the cities are mighty, ringed about by walls, stone fortresses which tower over the land! We have no weapons to tear down walls, nor rams to break their gates!"

And then others joined in. "The people are warriors, the sons of Anak, tall and broad-shouldered—men used to battle. The hills hold Hittites from the north, and Jebusites and Amorites. The coasts are the homes of Canaanites, and in the desert the Amalekites grow strong again!"

Only Caleb and Joshua spoke against them, reminding us of the Promise and of God's mighty power. They sought to assure the leaders of the tribes that God would give the land into our hands if only we would hold onto our faith and believe in and receive His gift.

But we didn't listen. *I* didn't listen. I was so caught up in my pride at Sethur's position in our tribe that I did not question his wisdom or dispute his judgment. As I heard him speak, I failed to recognize my father's sin—and my own—echoing in his words.

So when Sethur's words denied our faith, I did not think to question him. He and nine of the scouts went through the camp, speaking against the land of the Promise. As they spoke again of the cities' walls, they grew higher and thicker than mountains in our imagination. The Canaanites became warriors, then giants, then sons of demons, tall as towers and stronger than oxen.

❖

"We are grasshoppers in their sight," they wailed.

Perhaps we had been too long in Egypt, too used to cowering under Pharaoh's hand, too ready to accept whatever he deigned to give us, convinced that things could be otherwise. Perhaps we were too assured we could never be content, too quick to complain, too slow to hope, too faithless to believe.

Anyway, all of God's miracles, all the wonders we had seen, everything we *knew* to be true vanished from our sight. It was as if once again we were on the shores of the Red Sea, with Pharaoh's chariots thundering towards us and no faith at all that God could defeat our enemies, deliver us from bondage, and bless us with the gift of a Promised Land.

We were grasshoppers!

And we were fools! All night we wept, as if an enemy had fallen upon us, leaving our children slaughtered in the camps, whereas in truth not even an aged dog lay dead. Nothing had

17

changed; we had suffered no pestilence, we lacked no food, and our weapons were no less sharp than they had been the day before.

But suddenly all hope and confidence had vanished, leaving only disillusionment and fear. Some cried out for Egypt. Many cursed Moses or blamed God Himself, as if calamity were raining down from Heaven, though not even the edges of our tents so much as swayed in the wind.

There is no difference between faithlessness and fear, for both are blind.

A multitude of fools, we gathered before the Tent of Meeting, holding up torches in the night, looking this way and that as if threatening chariots of Canaan were lurking in the darkness beyond our camp. We shouted for Moses; and when he came out, we blamed him for the destruction of our families—families who still lay quite healthy and warm inside our tents.

Joshua and Caleb alone held onto their faith, rending their clothes in anguish for *our* lack of faith.

"The land we explored is exceedingly good!" they cried. "God will give it to us. Do not rebel against the Lord. Do not fear. We will swallow those people up, for their protection is gone and the Lord is with us!"

But we would not listen. Men began gathering stones, shouting threats at Joshua and Caleb as if they were murderers to be executed.

And then God came. The Glory of the Lord pierced through the Tent of Meeting like spears thrust through armor. His light seared through the night sky, making all our torches appear as nothing but embers in the grass. We dropped our stones and fell to the ground as we heard the Lord's terrible curse.

Move closer, Beriah. Can you lift the bowl to my lips yet one more time?

Now I am the last. They are all dead—everyone who feared

to follow the Lord's promise. Some died from the sword, trying to claim the Land of Promise without God. Some perished in the wilderness, some almost each day of the forty years that we wandered—forty years to remind us of our faithlessness.

Sethur and the other nine who had denied their faith were the first; I saw my son die, his face gone pale, his flesh devoured by a plague worse than all those that had humbled Pharaoh. Then the clan left our house, fleeing us as bearers of the Lord's curse, though in truth we all were lost. No longer did anyone seek wisdom from my lips, for there was none to be had.

On that day I remembered my grandmother's faith and my father's disdain for it. I too had followed my father's example, and my son had followed mine.

——————— ❖ ———————

I prayed, pleading with the Lord for forgiveness for my house, that my father's sin would be upon us no more.

And here you are, Beriah. After forty years, our tent sits again on the edge of Canaan. I know you have seen the green valleys and the forests on the hills. I no longer can. But I can smell the sweetness of distant grasses when the breeze rises from the north. The land is there, and it is good. I will never see it, nor will I taste its fruits. But it is good. It is the promise of the Lord.

Do you know that, Beriah? Do you trust the Lord? You never saw the miracles I witnessed, but you must believe more fervently than I ever did. *We* did not believe, Beriah. Though God was with us, though He led us and fought for us, we did not believe.

We thought we were grasshoppers, and grasshoppers we became. Do not be like we were, Beriah! *Believe the Lord.*

Have faith. We believed we were grasshoppers, but you must not!

I cannot hear you, Beriah. Are you there? My words grow faint; the light dims. We believed we were grasshoppers! You must not. You must not!

"Who's tent is that?" The young Israelite warrior jabbed the spearhead he had been grinding, back towards the mottled mass of cloth and hide on the edge of the camp. Holes, poorly mended, dotted across the coarse black walls of goat hair— looking more like a scattering of rags hung up to dry than a tent.

The other soldier glanced back, watching the tattered tent flap still swinging after he had left. "An old man named Mikhael, an Asherite who followed Moses from Egypt forty years ago. He kept calling me Beriah. He seemed to think that I was his grandson."

"Forty years ago! I thought the faithless ones had all died!"

Looking away towards the distant green valley lying far beyond the camp, the soldier nodded. "They all have," he said.

GOD'S WAY TO OVERCOME FEAR

Like Caleb and Joshua, we overcome fear and doubt by confronting them *immediately.*

Many people never conquer anxiety because they persist in dwelling on the cause of their fear. And as they wait longer and longer to act, the dread standing in their way grows larger and larger.

The time to overcome fear is the moment it attacks you. Just follow Caleb and Joshua's example by instantly responding to the "giant" through faith!

Caleb's declaration of belief didn't make him one of the most popular leaders in the tribe. Getting people to act through faith is difficult once they have been influenced by bad reports.

But Caleb saw his need to remain in the people's favor as secondary to his obligation and desire to please God.

———— ❖ ————

It isn't easy to confront adversity and work up the courage to stand up for what God has said when other people are telling you something else.

Then too, after you have overcome negative influences and have claimed what God has said, you may think the doubters and unbelievers will abandon their distrust. But as Caleb and Joshua discovered, this may not happen. Even after they spoke in support of their faith, the other scouts who had accompanied them protested, "We are not able to defeat these people, for they are stronger than we." Furthermore, they continued, "The land is full of men of great stature. We saw the giants, the sons of Anak, and we were in our sight as grasshoppers, and so we were in their sight."[1]

The ten scouts had much to overcome. They were struggling with fear, with the words of their mouths, and with doubt and unbelief. God had said He had given them the land, but the ten scouts doubted they could possess it. Instead of seeing the truth of God's promise in the huge grapes, they allowed their faith to be defeated by their fear of the giants.

THE REAL PROBLEM

But all these fears and doubts were only symptoms of the real problem: The ten scouts suffered from low self-esteem, or from *grasshopper mentality*.

You see, a person's perception of himself will dictate how he relates to other people. The doubting ten among the scouts had poor self-perception. They immediately assumed that everyone else saw them exactly as they saw themselves.

In one sense, of course, others *do* tend to perceive us the way we view ourselves. We actually project our own self-perception onto other people. So when we have a poor opinion of ourselves, we give off bad "vibes," so to speak, which can cause people to see us in the same negative way we see ourselves.

Before we go further, let me define "grasshopper mentality." Here are its symptoms:

- Having a small view of yourself
- Seeing yourself as insignificant and unimportant
- Having too acute a concern for your shortcomings and difficulties
- Having a feeling of inferiority which causes you to perceive everything that happens in your life as a reflection of what you cannot do or what you cannot be
- Thinking of yourself as a person who *can't* do something even before you try
- Viewing yourself as an individual who doesn't have what it takes to be more than average or, even worse, to be only average
- Looking in the mirror and seeing a reflection of someone you don't like very much
- Sizing things up and determining that you'll never get beyond where you are right now
- Being satisfied with a lifestyle in which mediocrity (being no more than average) is your goal
- A destructive second-rate feeling that makes you feel unqualified to be a vessel of God's goodness

If any of these symptoms describe the way you think, you may be suffering from grasshopper mentality.

SEEING OURSELVES AS GOD SEES US

Grasshopper mentality is a mindset which paralyzes, preventing us from being all God has called us to be. It is therefore a mindset from which the Lord doesn't intend for us to suffer. God wants us to think correctly—to see ourselves as He sees us, not through our faults and failures, as we so often do.

I'm always amazed by how many do nothing more than look for the standard that helps them to blend in with everyone else. They think if they can only manage to have a modest home, a car and a salary that pays their bills, a marriage that is all right most of the time and kids who earn average grades, they will be happy. But God hasn't called on His people to be average. He has called us to stand out.[2]

------------ ❖ ------------

We should never seek to be commonplace. We are called to stand in a class all by ourselves!

Consider again the words of the ten scouts: "And there we saw the giants, and we were in our own sight as grasshoppers."[3] These words reveal an important principle: *Assigning more importance to events and circumstances than to God's promises affects not only the way we think, but the way we see ourselves.* We come away with the negative conviction that confronted by the problems we face, we are no more than grasshoppers.

Magnifying our troubles tends to make us feel insignificant and valueless and traps us in this mentality—an unhealthy mindset controlled by thoughts of what we are unable to be or do.

THE RIGHT KIND OF "SMALL"

Grasshopper mentality fosters negatively limited thought that

23

is "small" thinking because it causes us to see ourselves as unimportant. But there is also a positive way to limit our thoughts—a desirable kind of "small" mentality, the type that allows us to embrace our total dependence on God, to gratefully accept the fact we are who we are, we have what we have, and we are destined to be what we become because of God's grace and love.

This is the kind of limited thinking that God wants us to have—quite different from the "small" thinking of grasshopper mentality which, by causing us to feel insignificant and impotent, prevents us from ever achieving, through faith, the greatness of which we are capable.

Many of us have long struggled to understand the true meaning of humility, sometimes falling into the error of assuming that in order to be humble, we have to think of ourselves as unimportant. But true humility is really only the recognition that all glory belongs to God. It is realizing He has led us to where we are, has blessed us with what we have, and will take us where He wants us to go.

With that difference in mind, I sometimes define grasshopper mentality this way: *It is to be small, but not like Saul.*

What do I mean by this statement? Before Saul became king of Israel, he had the right kind of small mentality. But once he wore the crown, he allowed himself to be overcome by pride, which eventually caused his downfall. In the Bible we learn how the prophet Samuel reminded Saul of what he once was like, telling him: *"Although you were once small in your own eyes, did you not become the head of the tribes of Israel? The Lord anointed you King over Israel."*[4]

Samuel was not implying that Saul, before becoming a king, had thought of himself as insignificant and lacking in self-esteem, but rather that he had been aware God's grace was the source of all he was and all he was destined to become.

Similarly, it was the ten negative scouts' Saul-like failure to take refuge in and strength from God's words and guidance that caused the attitude which led to their evil report.

God saw the ten scouts' report as evil for two reasons. The first being they said they *couldn't* when He said they *could*. They should have spoken of the *positive* things they had seen in the land, such as the large succulent grapes and rich produce; instead, they put their emphasis on *negative* details, like the giants.

The second reason their report was evil was because *they saw themselves as grasshoppers*. You displease the Lord when you think of yourself as small.

Here is why this kind of mentality is unacceptable to God:

- He created you in His image.
- He has empowered you with His strength.
- He has given you personal talents and abilities that reflect His image.
- He unhesitatingly sacrificed His only Son to redeem you.[5] He turned His back on Jesus on the cross, so He wouldn't have to turn His back on you.

When you fully grasp this, you can easily see why God is saddened and upset when you allow yourself to feel you are no more than a mere grasshopper. Failure to see yourself as everything God made you to be is *evil* in His eyes.

THE SYMPTOMS OF GRASSHOPPER MENTALITY

One major symptom of grasshopper mentality is the attitude that *no person should earn more than a certain amount of money*—a concept which may be encouraged by the deplorable tendency of our materialistic society to proclaim human worth in material terms with limiting evaluations such as: "Fred is worth no more than a few thousand dollars, but his brother Mike is worth more than ten million." Such an attitude toward Fred is typical "you're-never-going-to-be-anything-great" thinking, which is tantamount to accepting an insurmountable fixed limitation on the value of a human life.

Society is wrong to impose a monetary value on humanity. But we would be equally wrong to apply the corollary of this notion on ourselves—the negative belief that we shouldn't earn more money—and thereby "value ourselves"—beyond a certain limit. Should we ever feel hindered by the negative feeling that we have reached "maximum worth" in our lives? Of course, not.

Another grasshopper symptom is the false sense of humility described earlier, especially when problems arise. Thinking of themselves as just being humble and insignificant they belittle their ability by making statements such as, "This problem is just too big for me to overcome." But they are only conditioning themselves to be defeated at everything they set their hands to do, thereby ensuring they will never enter their personal "promised lands."

When we adopt such thinking we allow ourselves to be more attuned to our shortcomings and difficulties than to the positive attributes with which God has blessed us.

———— ❖ ————

The Lord wants us to understand that through Christ Jesus we are repositories for everything good life can provide.

Grasshopper mentality prevents people from understanding this and blocks them from knowing how to receive God's love. He may try to bless them, but they shun Him and push away the blessing because they feel unworthy to receive it. Instead, they try to *earn* God's love. They rationalize that if they do good deeds today and during the rest of the week, God will love them enough to answer their prayers.

Sadly, this is how many people think God operates. But such thinking directly contradicts the teaching of the Holy Scripture, which tells us, "God demonstrated His own love for us in this: that while we were still sinners Christ died for us."[6] This Scripture plainly tells us that God is never going to love us any more than He already does.

Of course, you still need to let God work in your life to make you better. You should still allow Him to cleanse you of any impurities and take you to the next level in Him. But even as you grow in God, His love for you doesn't change. He still loves you exactly the same. And the knowledge that Almighty God's love for you is consistent establishes your self-worth. It changes your countenance and your disposition. It alters the way you walk, the way you talk, the way you interact with others, and the way you carry on your daily affairs. This is why it is so important that you stop thinking you have *earned* God's love and begin receiving His unconditional love through faith!

LEAVE A LEGACY BEHIND

Grasshoppers are also different from More Than Conquerors because *they never leave a mark on life*. Only those who have the right mentality can leave a legacy behind. To understand what this means, just think back to the account in Numbers 13 and answer these questions:

1. What was the name of the leader who led the children of Israel out of Egypt? (Moses)
2. Where were they going? (Canaan)
3. How many scouts were sent to evaluate the land? (Twelve)
4. How many came back with a good report? (Two)

5. How many came back with a bad report? (Ten)
6. What were the names of those who brought back the good report? (Joshua and Caleb)
7. What were the names of those who brought back the bad report?

You can probably answer the first six questions, but not the seventh. We fail to remember their names, even though the Bible tells us who they were, because grasshopper mentality blocked them from both achievement and recognition. They didn't achieve because of a breach of faith. Instead of embracing the truth that all of us are potentially capable of greatness because God created us, they sold themselves short, crippled by a feeling of inferiority which told them they couldn't do what God had told them they *could* do.

So the names of the ten scouts are never mentioned in Sunday school or from the preacher's pulpit because people with no vision never leave a mark. We tend to see them as they saw themselves.

In a sense, the story of the human race is an account of men and women selling themselves short. Most people never pursue and develop their potential talents and abilities. Even in the Church, many individuals don't see who they are in Christ, thinking they are pleasing God by being humble.

Now that we have a better understanding of how God feels about grasshopper mentality, consider how annoyed He must have been with the response Moses made to His command to go back to Egypt and set His people free: "I can't go and speak on Your behalf, Lord. I am not articulate enough. They won't listen to me."

The Bible records how *the anger of the Lord was kindled* against Moses when he sold himself short.[7]

God is eternal. He is the same now as He was then. If He

calls you to do something on His behalf, He expects you to believe you are *more* than a conqueror in all things.[8] You displease God if you lack faith and don't believe in yourself.

ALWAYS CARRY A GOOD REPORT IN YOUR HEART

A fourth characteristic of grasshoppers is *their tendency to carry a bad report*, whereas More Than Conquerors always possess a good report. Grasshoppers are consistently blocked from achievement by thoughts of what might go wrong. But significant success would never be possible if we allowed ourselves to be put off through fear of hypothetical obstacles.

If God has placed a dream in your heart, you first need to savor the brightness of the vision. For the moment, forget *how* to go about accomplishing your task. The "how" is not important in the initial consideration of the dream. Just focus on the vision and develop it until it is so bright that all potential obstacles pale in comparison. Then, motivated by the vision and strengthened by faith in your ability to make it a reality, consider and tackle all the obstacles.

This is how to approach and accomplish a God-given dream. Envision the dream—what God wants you to do—in its entirety.

————— ❖ —————

The Lord sees problems just as you do, but from His vantage point they are small and easy to overcome.

Instead of first focusing on what makes a dream worth pursuing, too many people let themselves be put off by potential problems. But nothing good can ever be accomplished by this kind of an approach.

As you can see, grasshoppers are perpetual incubators of bad

29

news—reports which are misguided by fear rather than reached through faith. Good reports reflect what God wants us to do and has assured us is possible.

The Lord wants us to birth *glad* tidings. When called upon to give testimonies in their churches, too many people fail to understand what constitutes a positive witness. Someone might say, for instance, "I thank God that I burned my arm, because the injury gave me an opportunity to witness to the doctor!"

The Greek word for "report" is synonymous with "testimony." The person who gave the report (or "testimony") concerning his burn failed to understand the difference between recognizing how God can bring good out of a bad situation and praising God for allowing his arm to be burned. The Bible tells us that all things work together for the good for those who love God and are called according to His purpose.[9] But it *doesn't* tell us that God is the *originator* of all things.

Jesus told us exactly where both good and bad stem from when He said: *"The thief does not come except to steal, and to kill, and to destroy. I have come that they may have life, and that they may have it more abundantly."*[10] The Bible tells us our Father is a caring God whose gifts are consistently good. Nowhere are we told that He also inflicts bad or evil on us just because He *can*.

Only *good* comes from the Father, for He is a God of life. So when you hold the hope of a good report in your heart, you become an incubator of life. And as this grows within you, you change entirely, and your countenance reflects such a transformation.

ASSOCIATE WITH INCUBATORS OF GOOD REPORTS

When we begin to foster a bad report by letting our minds

dwell on negative things, we can become depressed. Our countenance changes, as does our physical appearance. Even our health may deteriorate. This is why associating with incubators of what is good is so imperative. Those we surround ourselves with either help us remain grasshoppers by reinforcing negative news or help us overcome this mentality by challenging us with the truth of God's Word. So if we find that the people with whom we associate aren't challenging us to improve, we probably need to distance ourselves from them.

———— ❖ ————

Cultivate relationships which inspire you to rise to the next level in God.

The power of association can be vividly seen in the life of Helen Keller. On the advice of Dr. Alexander Graham Bell, the parents of Miss Keller sent for a teacher from the Perkins Institution for the Blind in Boston to help their troubled daughter. To her parents' dismay, little Helen, as a result of not knowing how to deal with her blindness, would often fall into fits of rage. In response to their cry for help, the Institution sent Anne Sullivan, a nineteen-year-old orphan, with the task of instructing six-year-old Helen.

It was the beginning of a close and lifelong friendship between them. By means of a manual alphabet, Anne "spelled" words such as *doll* or *puppy* into Helen's hand. Two years later, Helen, who at one time had seemed destined for illiteracy, was reading and writing Braille fluently. At ten, she learned different sounds by placing her fingers on her teacher's larynx and "hearing" the vibrations. Later, she attended Radcliffe College, where Anne spelled the lectures into Helen's hand. And after graduating with honors, Helen decided to devote her life to helping the blind and deaf. As part of this endeavor, she wrote many books and articles and traveled around the world lecturing. Since Helen's speeches were not intelligible to some, Anne often translated them for her.

After their nearly fifty years of companionship ended with Anne's death in 1936, Helen wrote these endearing words about her lifelong friend:

"My teacher is so near to me that I scarcely think of myself apart from her. I feel that her being is inseparable from my own, and that the footsteps of my life are in hers. All the best of me belongs to her—there is not a talent or an inspiration or a joy in me that has not been awakened by her loving touch."[11]

As Helen's story illustrates, our outlook is often affected by those with whom we choose to associate. And just as Anne's strongly positive attitude inspired a similar perspective in Helen, those trapped in grasshopper mentality infect others with their limited view.

Ralph Waldo Emerson once observed, "What people need most is someone to make them do what they can do." This is why even the best professional athletes need coaches. God has gifted the athletes with great talent and athletic potential, but they need coaches to encourage and inspire them to do what God has made it *possible* for them to accomplish.

And all of us need the same sort of positive encouragement from our close friends; people in our lives whose uplifting influence will help us reach our goals.

Mark Twain also understood this need. "Keep away from people who try to belittle your ambitions," he advised. Only small people torpedo others' aspirations. Those who are truly outstanding motivate us to see that we too can become great.

One of my objectives each Sunday when I share God's Word with my congregation is to try to make each person leave thinking he or she can conquer the world.

If you're not inclined to accept Emerson or Twain's advice,

perhaps a more direct admonition from the *Bible* will prove more persuasive: *"Do not be deceived: Bad company corrupts good morals."*[12] In other words, if you consort with people who are grasshoppers, you may find yourself corrupted by their bad report.

———— ❖ ————

You'll never enjoy an overcoming life until you decide to stand up to the negativity and be counted among those who believe God's Word more than external circumstances!

DON'T BE DISCOURAGED BY WHAT YOU DON'T HAVE

A fifth symptom of grasshopper mentality is a tendency to obsess unproductively over what one *doesn't have*. More Than Conquerors are more inclined to be grateful for what they *do* possess.

A Bible story involving that characteristic of grasshopper mentality concerns the woman whom God commanded to sustain Elijah during a great famine.[13] The Almighty spoke, telling her to take care of and sustain Elijah. But the woman hesitated over the divine command because of her concern that she might not have enough food to provide for herself and her son. When Elijah went to the woman's home and asked for something to eat, instead of obeying God's directive, she cried out, "As the Lord thy God liveth, I have not a cake, but an handful of meal in a barrel, and a little oil in a cruse: and, behold, I am gathering two sticks, that I may go in and dress it for me and my son, that we may eat it, and die." The woman's response to God's will was blocked by her fears concerning what she did not have.

Fortunately, Elijah was able to help the woman move beyond her grasshopper mentality by boldly assuring her that if she gave him a bite to eat first, God would increase what she had in order to provide amply for both herself and her son.

We all know how concerned we can become when God asks us to give more than we think we can afford. The Lord desires to give rather than take, but before He can do this, He needs a seed to work with that has been sown by faith. Thank God Elijah was able to help the woman break away from her narrow thinking so she could receive her miracle!

Grasshopper mentality will *always* cause you to miss your blessing, and this is why you need to surround yourself with people who will shake you out of this limited way of thinking. You need to pray for some Elijahs to come into your life!

KEEP FOCUSED ON THE JOY SET BEFORE YOU

A sixth sign of this mentality is that *grasshoppers are always looking back*, whereas those who are More Than Conquerors have their eyes on the prize. Their focus is on the future.

———— ❖ ————

You can't drive fast down a highway while looking in the rearview mirror.

Similarly, you can't move forward in life while dwelling in the past. Looking back will either slow you down or entirely halt your progress.

Not long ago on a hot summer day, my then seven-year-old daughter Nicole and I were racing in our backyard swimming pool, and I was letting her win. She got way out ahead of me, then suddenly turned her head to look back.

I yelled, "Hey, don't look back, Honey! Keep going!"

because I wanted her to win the race. But as soon as she turned to see where I was, she began to veer off course and slow down.

Grasshoppers have this same tendency, compromising any progress they may have made. They mirror Lot's wife. And you know what happened to her. She turned into a pillar of salt!

It seems significant that Lot's wife was turned into a *pillar* of salt—a solid, immovable *block*. We are called upon to be "the salt of the earth," but here it is meant to be an *attractive* seasoning which draws people toward the Lord. This can only happen if our salt remains fluid, moving forward. When grasshoppers look back instead of forward, they turn into stationary salt "pillars," unable to influence anyone else for God's Kingdom. On the other hand, More Than Conquerors always look *forward*, like Jesus, who set His face like a flint toward the joy set *before* Him, enduring the Cross.[14]

DON'T LIVE ON BORROWED DREAMS

The seventh characteristic of grasshoppers is that they live on *borrowed* dreams. More Than Conquerors give birth to their *own* dreams and then do whatever is necessary to bring them to fulfillment.

Personal goals are vitally important. You have to have a dream ahead of you in order to move forward toward maturity. God, in fact, intended you to be motivated by something in front of you. The Bible tells us God doesn't push. He *draws* us. As Jesus said, *"And I, if I be lifted up from the earth, will DRAW all men unto me."*[15]

Dreams have this same effect on us: they keep pulling us forward. One little boy's aspiration to walk on the moon illustrates the inherent power of dreams. It started as do so many evenings—Mom and Dad at home and Jimmy playing after dinner. Absorbed in their own thoughts and activities, Mom and

Dad didn't notice the time. The moon was full, and some of the light seeped through the windows. Then Mom glanced at the clock. "Jimmy, it's time to go to bed. Go up now, and I'll come and settle you later." Uncharacteristically, Jimmy went straight upstairs to his room without protesting. But when, an hour or so later, his mother came up to see if all was well, to her astonishment she found her son staring quietly out of his window at the moonlit scenery.

"What are you doing, Jimmy?"

"I'm looking at the moon, Mommy."

"Well, it's time to go to bed."

When Jimmy reluctantly settled down, he commented, "Mommy, you know—one day I'm going to walk on the moon."

Jimmy grew and held this dream in his heart, so that as an adult, even after surviving a near-fatal motorbike crash in which he broke almost every bone in his body, threatening his ability ever to walk again. This man, James Irwin, was able to triumph over adversity and turn his dream into reality by actually stepping onto the moon's surface to become one of only twelve individuals to do so.[16] This is the potential power of a dream!

———— ❖ ————

Keep looking forward toward the vision
God has planted in your heart.

If you try to live out someone else's dream, you will quickly lose interest because it is not really yours. If it is, however, you'll never have to doubt its validity, and your own passion for its fulfillment will carry you through every storm.

Of course, this is not to say you can't ever share a dream that others have. But God created all of us as unique individuals with special destinies, so you must be sure that your dream, no matter how many other people may *share* it, is really *yours*, rather than something you have just *borrowed.*

DON'T LET PASSING CIRCUMSTANCES DICTATE WHAT YOU WILL ACCEPT IN LIFE

The eighth grasshopper tendency is to allow *passing or temporary circumstances* to dictate what one accepts in life. More Than Conquerors let their actual desire determine what they accept.

When ordering in a restaurant, for example, a grasshopper will read the menu from right to left and order by *price* rather than choosing what he or she would really *like* to have, settling for the untempting "$3.95 Special" even if there are mouth-watering favorites available. In this instance, the grasshopper is allowing a passing circumstance—the current state of personal finances—to determine what he or she will choose.

You should allow your *desires* to dictate what you want from life. I don't mean desires of the *flesh*, of course, but rather those *God* has inspired in you. More Than Conquerors know that the dreams they pursue should be motivated by the passion God has placed within them.

EMBRACE CHANGE AS THE PATH TO PROGRESS

Characteristic nine is that *grasshoppers tend to be afraid of change because it threatens their fragile sense of security.* On the other hand, More Than Conquerors understand how change is a necessary element of progress.

I like the way a man from the back mountains of Tennessee embraced change. One day, accompanied by his young son, he found himself in a large city and, for the first time, standing in front of an elevator—a contraption the likes of which he had never seen before. He watched as a haggard old woman hobbled into the elevator and the door closed. Then, when a few minutes later the door opened again and a young, attractive woman walked smartly out, he yelled to his son, "Billy, go get mother!"[17]

———— ❖ ————

Change can be a wonderful instrument of progress when it is welcomed.

Regrettably, though, grasshoppers register concern when you talk about this issue, but their worry is centered on how it affects them *personally*—an attitude which shows them to be pridefully self-serving. In contrast, More Than Conquerors know that it isn't just all about *them*.

Change is the key that opens doors. Failure to use the key traps us in our past, whereas using it releases us to seek our destiny.

FIND REASONS TO SUCCEED, NOT EXCUSES FOR FAILURE

The tenth identifying tendency of grasshoppers is to allow potential obstacles to become excuses for not moving forward. On the other hand, More Than Conquerors understand that progress *always* involves risk and getting ahead is impossible unless you're courageous enough to *take* chances. There will always be imagined reasons why you can't enter your Promised Land. There will always be giants and other obstacles standing in your way. So you have to decide whether you will let yourself be immobilized by the fear of *giants*, or energized by the promise of *grapes*.

The story is told of two salesmen who went to the Australian outback to sell shoes to the Aborigines. The first salesman arrived a week early, disembarked from the plane, and met with his prospective customers. He noticed immediately, to his horror, that they didn't *wear* shoes. Discouraged, he took the next flight home after sending a telegram to his office that read, "Bad idea, Aborigines don't wear shoes."

The following week the second salesman arrived and was thrilled at what he saw. He immediately set up shop and sent a telegram to *his* home office saying, "Send all the shoes you can, Aborigines don't have any!"

We determine whether we will fail or flourish by how we approach life—by whether we trap ourselves in doubt and unbelief or move ahead, strengthened and motivated by faith. We need to find reasons for doing what God expects of us instead of finding excuses for our inaction.

PRAISE GOD BEFORE YOU EXPERIENCE HIS BLESSINGS

An eleventh characteristic of grasshoppers is *the mistake of questioning and blaming God*, while More Than Conquerors *praise God even in adversity because of their faith in His unwavering goodness!*

Consider the example of Paul and Silas, who were beaten for preaching the Gospel. Many people would ask, "Why did you let this happen to me, God? I was only doing what You told me to do! I was preaching the Gospel, and this is what I get for it! What kind of God are You anyway?"

But instead of grumbling over their mistreatment, the two men praised God in spite of their suffering. And as a result, the Lord intervened on their behalf through an earthquake. The jail began to shake, the apostles' bonds were broken, and they found themselves set free!

The story of Paul and Silas is a prime example of the

thinking of More than Conquerors, who are always ready for the next task God has planned for them. After overcoming a challenge, they want to get right back to pursuing what the Lord has called them to do. And they consistently praise God even in adversity and give Him all the glory in times of triumph!

Grasshoppers, on the other hand, walk by *sight* and not by *faith*. But the information we receive through our natural sense of sight is demonstrably limited. For example, a small amount of drinking water in a Petri dish looks clear to the naked eye. But if you put a drop of the same water under a microscope, you'll discover that your sight was quite deficient, for there are actually living, moving microorganisms in the water. Our sight obviously doesn't tell us the whole story.

---- ❖ ----

People who have learned to depend on faith understand the limits of our natural vision, and this is why they look through the eyes of faith to find God's perspective on all things.

The book of Second Kings provides an insightful lesson concerning the comparative merits of human sight and seeing through the eyes of faith. It tells of an encounter between the great prophet of God, Elisha, and the king of Syria. The king had become enraged at Elisha because he continually warned the king of Israel of Syria's war plans to attack Israel, thereby spoiling the operation before it could be put into action. So Syria sent hosts of horses and chariots to encompass the whole city where Elijah was, planning to destroy both it and the prophet.

When Elisha's servant saw the great army surrounding the city, he became terribly frightened and wondered aloud how Israel could escape. But Elisha looked at the situation through the eyes of faith, seeing God's angelic hosts encircling their adversary. So he prayed that God would open the eyes of his servant. And the Lord did, whereupon the young man looked again and saw that this time the mountain was full of divinely sent horses and chariots of fire in greater number than those of Syria's army.[18]

Two observers saw entirely different things! The servant was looking at what he could see only with his physical sight. The person whom he served was looking through the eyes of faith.

This story illustrates how *our station in life is dependent on the lens through which we look*. However, a distinction needs to be made between *station* in life and *position* in life. As Jesus said, *"He that is greatest among you shall be your servant.*[19] A person may have the *position* of servant while having a much higher *station* in life at the same time. If God has placed you under someone else's authority, He has you in that position so you can learn how to see through the eyes of faith. Joshua serves as a good illustration of this principle. He was Moses' servant long before he led the children of Israel into the Promised Land.

During those years of preparation, Joshua never went up to Moses and exclaimed, "Moses, you don't have it right this time. You're not seeing the situation correctly." Joshua understood how the Lord had placed him under Moses' authority so that the faith God was developing in Moses might inspire a similar belief in *him* and equip him to lead God's people after Moses was gone.

The account of Moses and Joshua reveals another important principle. If you embrace the life role that God has given you and begin to see through the eyes of faith, you can become an even better leader than the person under whose authority God has placed you. Moses couldn't lead the children of Israel into the Promised Land, but Joshua could.

CULTIVATE INNER IMAGES
BASED ON GOD'S WORD

The twelfth symptom of grasshopper mentality is that *a grasshopper cultivates images projected by the enemy*, whereas a More Than Conqueror nourishes images God reveals to him.

You see, it's as if the devil has a camera crew who secretly follow you everywhere. Whenever you do something you shouldn't, the demonic camera crew is snapping photos to put into Satan's photo album. Then, the moment you reach the outskirts of Canaan, the enemy opens the photo album and announces, "Do you think yourself fit to inherit your Promised Land? Don't you know that it's reserved only for those who have never messed up? Take a look at your actions. We caught you red-handed, you rascal!"

The devil understands that the center of man's creative genius is his ability to see images with the power of imagination. He understands the way Second Corinthians 10:5 operates, and he works it in reverse: *Casting down arguments and every high thing that exalts itself against the knowledge of God, bringing every thought into captivity to the obedience of Christ.*

God also understands the power of your imagination. He created you with this ability so you can experience the fullness of His promises! To be sure, when you reach the border of your personal Promised Land, the devil will try to trap you with the image of a particular giant of which he wants you to be afraid. But you must not focus on this! Instead, use your imagination to destroy it in favor of a faith image from God's photo album!

Yes, God has a camera crew too. But His angelic photographers catch you every time you do something *right*. The Lord keeps a record of the positive because, as the Bible tells us, one day you will be rewarded for your good works.[20]

On the same topic, there are two things God wants us to remember: First, the damage recorded in the devil's photo album is not permanent. According to the Bible, if you ask God to forgive you, He doesn't even *remember* your iniquities.[21] This means the images of your past sins in Satan's photo album are only illusory, because God has wiped them away and forgotten they ever existed!

Second, God doesn't keep His photos of our good deeds only in an album; He also emblazons them on a battle flag —a standard.[22]

———— ❖ ————

God's power is more of a flooding force in your life than the enemy's strategy against you could ever possibly be.

The mighty standard God raises up is a banner full of all your past victories—everything you have personally accomplished for His Kingdom. Right at the top of this banner is a picture of the Cross and of an empty tomb, because everything Jesus accomplished in the work of redemption has been credited to your account.

Colossians 2:18 tells us, *"Let no man therefore beguile you* [trick you] *of your reward..."* This is what the devil is trying to accomplish with his false images. But never forget that you have a standard backed up by Jesus! Everything He did is just as if *you* had done it yourself.

So remember, the photo album the devil keeps in order to show you your past failures and sins is really an illusion. God's banner, which displays who you are and what you have in Christ, is the standard by which you need to live. Don't be a grasshopper who cultivates images based only on the pictures the devil shows you. Focus on faith images like those on the standard of truth which *God* continually raises up.

When you are at the outskirts of your Canaan and the devil displays his photo album full of giants and seemingly insurmountable walls, visualize the enormous grapes awaiting you in your Promised Land. They represent *God's* promise for your life in Him. Only you can decide which image to cultivate in your heart.

PURSUE YOUR DESTINY THROUGH FAITH

The thirteenth grasshopper tendency *is to* hope *to be in the right place at the right time.* More Than Conquerors know that destiny is not a matter of chance; it is a matter of *choice.* It isn't something to be waited for, rather something to be *achieved.*

---------- ❖ ----------

Far too many people walk around thinking if they can just be in the right place at the right time, all will go well for them. But such a mindset is the product of pure grasshopper mentality.

More Than Conquerors understand that time and chance happen to *all,*[23] even if opportunity sometimes knocks in curious ways, as Steve Jobs illustrates:

"I was lucky. I found what I loved to do early in life. Woz (Steve Wozniak) and I started Apple in my parent's garage when I was twenty. We worked hard, and in ten years Apple had grown from just the two of us in a garage to a two-billion-dollar company with over 4,000 employees. We had just released our finest creation, the Macintosh, a year earlier, and I had just turned thirty. And then I got fired. How can you get fired from a company you started? Well, as Apple grew, we hired someone who I thought was very talented to run the company with me, and for the first year or so things went well. But then our visions of the future began to diverge, and eventually we had a falling out. When we did, our Board of Directors sided with him. So at thirty I was out. And very publicly out. What had been the focus of my entire adult life was gone, and it was devastating.

"I didn't see it then, but it turned out that getting fired from Apple was the best thing that could have ever happened to me. The heaviness of being successful was replaced by the lightness of being a beginner again, less sure about everything. It freed me to enter one of the most creative periods in my life.

"During the next five years, I started a company named NeXT, another company named Pixar, and fell in love with an amazing woman who would become my wife. Pixar went on to create the world's first computer-animated feature film, *Toy Story*, and is now the most successful animation Studio in the world. In a remarkable turn of events, Apple bought NeXT, I returned to Apple, and the technology we developed at NeXT is at the heart of Apple's current renaissance. And Laurene and I have a wonderful family together.

"I'm pretty sure none of this would have happened if I hadn't been fired from Apple. It was awful tasting medicine, but I guess the patient needed it."[24]

This is a classic example of seeing life through the eyes of a More Than Conqueror—realizing that you and I must seize the moment and take hold of the opportunities which come our way, even when they appear in a form that is quite unusual.

In other words, More Than Conquerors understand that everyone is in the right place at the right time *some* of the time. But even when the right place and the right time come together, the grasshopper continues to wait for *God* to do something. In contrast, the More Than Conqueror says, "I'm stepping out in faith and riding on the wave God is sending my way!"

If you want to rid yourself of wrong thinking, recognize

those situations when the right time and the right place come together to present you with an open door to opportunity. Then you must take advantage of the moment regardless of the challenges!

Finally, here are a few summarizing illustrations that distinguish grasshoppers from More Than Conquerors:

- Grasshoppers don't know their purpose, whereas More Than Conquerors do.
- Grasshoppers overemphasize the sovereignty of God. They live their lives *hoping* that their mountains will move. More Than Conquerors live their lives believing their mountains will move.
- Grasshoppers abandon their vision when others don't share it. More Than Conquerors understand that not everyone will embrace their vision.
- Grasshoppers are afraid to take risks and instead tend to choose their comfortable status quo. More Than Conquerors accept challenges and make deliberate and courageous movements toward change.
- Grasshoppers think of obstacles as too big to overcome because they see themselves as small. Hurdles seem manageably small to More Than Conquerors because they have a positive self-image and understand who they are in God's eyes.
- Because grasshoppers live without convictions, they have no motivation. Because More Than Conquerors are people of principle, they are inner-driven. They understand that it isn't what they live for that really matters, but what they are prepared to die for.
- Grasshoppers suffer from *the paralysis of analysis*. More Than Conquerors understand that with each bold step comes more revelation.

- Grasshoppers tend to be satisfied with their past successes. More Than Conquerors understand that if they are going to live successful lives, they have to try to outdo themselves every day.

We should never let ourselves be content with where we are at any given moment. Instead, we must continually press on to achieve higher marks and attain greater heights in God, overcoming grasshopper mentality by disciplining our minds through faith to see ourselves through God's eyes.

CHAPTER TWO

CREATING AN OVERCOMER ENVIRONMENT

T hink again of the ten scouts' negative report: *"We were like grasshoppers in our own sight, and so we were in their sight."*[1] Since the Hebrew word for grasshopper also means *locust*, we can further understand the effects of grasshopper mentality by considering a few facts concerning locusts.

Fact One: Scientists have learned that when food is scarce under certain climatic conditions, chemical changes take place in female locusts which cause more eggs to hatch than normal. When this happens, gigantic swarms of locusts fill the air in search of food.

This is very significant for our study of grasshopper mentality because it tells us we need to change the climatic conditions in our lives that allow the eggs of such a debilitating mentality to hatch, replacing it with an atmosphere in which a More Than Conqueror mentality can flourish.

So we need to think on how to alter our own environment so negative seeds already sown in our lives through people,

49

circumstances, or other means are no longer allowed to spring forth. Later we will consider some "climate control principles" —ways in which we can regulate our atmosphere in order to change our thinking.

Fact Two: Farmers dread locusts because they destroy crops and foliage in large areas.

Just remember the total devastation which occurred in Egypt when Pharaoh refused to free God's people and the Lord sent the plague of locusts upon the land!

We face a similarly destructive plague.

—————— ❖ ——————

A poor self-image will destroy everything to which you set your hand.

You may say, "But the Bible declares everything I set my hand to will prosper." But this won't happen with wrong thinking because it will prevent you from achieving anything greater than the limit imposed on you by the small negative image you have of yourself.

Fact Three: A locust plague is virtually impossible to stop.

When an attempt is made, for instance, to drown swarms of devastating locusts, the survivors just use the bodies of the dead ones as a bridge to walk over the surface of the water!

So what is God telling us through this particular characteristic of the locust? When people with this mentality begin to lose the good things in their lives such as relationships, financial security, and favor with others, they often don't perceive their losses as a wakeup call. They fail to rebound with

"Hey, I need to find out why this is happening and do something about it!" Instead, "excuse-ism" sets in, and they permit excuses to prevent them from seeking remedies and moving forward—including: *I can never get ahead because nobody likes me; I just can't catch a break; I'm just not smart enough; I'm not good-looking enough; I don't know the right people, or I'm not of the right ethnicity.*

All these rationales build and enforce a stronghold in a grasshopper's mind that is impossible to tear down without bringing the power of God's Word to bear on the situation. Otherwise this becomes a debilitating substitute for constructive action, blocking the realization that no matter what an individual's external characteristics and circumstances may be, he or she has God on the inside as an empowerment to greatness.

Fact Four: Locusts are known to smother the fires that are sent to destroy them.

This suggests God will send revival fires to our hearts. But when we have grasshopper mentality, we don't respond to the wakeup call and allow the fires to revive us. And unless we rid ourselves of negative thinking we will never permit the fire of the Spirit to fulfill its purpose.

Fact Five: The only way to get rid of locusts is to poison them and destroy the females' eggs before they can hatch.

What is the antidote we can use? *The truth of God's Word.* You can eliminate destructive thinking by replacing old thoughts of doubt and unbelief with what Scripture declares. You must destroy those deadly "eggs" that you've been incubating within before they hatch!

How do we do this? And how can we create an environment in which we can nurture a More Than Conqueror mentality?

Let's consider some "climate control principles" that will help us answer these questions. We've already touched on the first principle, which is simply: *We must take control of our thoughts.* God speaks to us on this subject in Second Corinthians, where He tells us to cast down imaginings and take control of our thoughts.[2]

Remember, the word "imaginings" refers to those pictures we have developed in our minds, either based on the enemy's lies or on God's Word.

It is surprising how people can hold onto obviously false perceptions concerning situations or subjects. In the past something must have happened in these individual's lives; perhaps a small seed of a lie was sown in their minds, upon which they fixated until it finally became a vain figment of imagination with the destructive force of a swarm of locusts.

This is why God has told us to cast down vain imaginings and embrace what is good based on His Word. But just what *is* a good imagining?

- To envision yourself as God sees you.
- To envision yourself conquering a particular area of weakness.
- To envision yourself walking in all He has for you.
- To envision yourself experiencing your God-given dream.

These are the positive views you need to nurture by means of a steady diet of the Word.

One thing is certain—the Scriptures certainly teach us that we have the ability to take control of our thoughts. God wouldn't tell us to clear our minds of what is wrong if we were unable to do so. If the task were impossible, He would just be setting us up to spin our wheels and become frustrated. But with God's help, we can accomplish the task.

There are two very important reasons why we need to take command of our thoughts:

Reason One: *We are what we* think *we are.*[3] One farmer's experience with an eaglet makes this clear. While walking through the forest one day, he found a young eaglet which had fallen out of its nest. He took it home and put it in the barnyard with his chickens, where it spent so much time with its new companions that it began to think it *was* a chicken—eating and behaving just like them.

One day a naturalist who passed by the farm asked why the king of all birds was confined to living in the barnyard with chickens. The farmer explained that since he had given it chicken feed and trained it to be a chicken; it had never learned to fly.

"Surely it can be taught, " replied the naturalist. He lifted the eagle toward the heavens and announced, "You belong to the sky and not to the earth. Flap your wings and fly!"

The eagle was confused, not knowing what to do. So still thinking it was a chicken and seeing its companions eating their food, it jumped out of his grip to be with them again.

Undaunted, the naturalist then took the bird to the roof of the farmhouse and said: "You are an eagle. Stretch your wings and fly." But the bird, looking around and seeing nothing else but chickens pecking at their food, jumped down once more to join them.

Still persisting, the naturalist finally removed the eagle from the barnyard entirely and carried it to the top of a high mountain, where he held the king of birds high above his head and encouraged it once more: "You are an eagle."

This time the bird looked towards the sky, then back toward the barnyard, wrestling with its thoughts. Finally, the eagle stretched its wings and with a confident and triumphant cry, soared high into the heavens.[4]

The baby eaglet had to struggle to become what it was born to be because its perception of its native uniqueness had been blocked by the mediocrity of the environment.

The same is true with you and me. We can never be more than we think we are. So, if we have been born to fly like eagles, but for whatever reason are inclined to think like chickens, we must strive to triumph over such limited imaginings.

More Than Conquerors know that as a man thinks in his heart, so is he. As the French philosopher Descartes reasoned, *"Je pense, donc je suis"*—I think, therefore I am.

Reason Two: *The mind is the primary battlefield on which the Devil can threaten our lives.* As Second Corinthians tells us, *"Lest Satan should get an advantage of us: for we are not ignorant of his devices."*[5]

Author Rick Renner, who is well known for his extensive knowledge of New Testament Greek, says this about the word "devices": It is a translation of the Greek word *noemata* (no-e-ma-ta), which is derived from the word *nous* (pronounced *no-ous*), and *nous* is the Greek word for the *mind* or the *intellect*. Paul's use of the word *noemata* in Second Corinthians carries out the idea of a *deceived* mind. Specifically, it denotes Satan's insidious and malevolent plot to fill the human mind with confusion.[6]

God is telling us that Satan doesn't have an advantage in our lives unless we give it to him. And the only way he can gain this leverage is to deceive us into improper thinking. Distracting our minds through deception is Satan's favorite stratagem. He uses it at every turn because he knows it is the only way he can influence us. And this, of course, is why God commands us to cast down vain imaginings and refuse to foster them.

CLIMATE CONTROL PRINCIPLE #1
RENOVATE YOUR THINKING WITH GOD'S WORD

Taking control of our thoughts is vitally important in establishing the right climate for overcomer mentality. First we must analyze our thought processes and examine the nature of them; then we must seriously commit ourselves to renewing our minds. One of the best ways to renovate our thinking is to re-program our thoughts with the truth of God's Word. Romans 12:2 comments on this approach: *And do not be conformed to this world, but be transformed by the renewing of your mind, that you may prove what is that good and acceptable and perfect will of God.*

This verse reveals powerful insight on how to overcome grasshopper mentality. First, *"Don't think according to the world's system."* Those trapped in this are ensnared because their thinking is restricted by such a mindset. They are the ones who insist, "You can't do that" or "If you haven't been able to do it in the past, you won't be able to do it now, and you certainly won't be able to do it in the future."

———— ❖ ————

We can always find reasons and excuses for failure, but God doesn't want us to wallow in pessimism.

He shows us another way: *by renewing our minds with His truth.* We have to *renovate our thinking* by tearing down the old and putting in the new.

Instead of reinforcing all of the reasons why we can't, God's Word inspires within us a "can do" attitude which is instrumental to overcoming small thinking. It admonishes us we can do all things,[7] that all things are possible,[8] and with God's help we are destined to win![9]

The book of Romans gives us a second requirement to help us overcome grasshopper mentality. *We are to renovate our thinking by knowing the will of God.*[10] Many fail to harness the power of their thoughts because they apparently assume they can *never* know God's will. Their prayers testify to this misconception, often beseeching God to do this or that with the qualifying phrase: *"If it be Thy will."*

But the Bible tells us God wants us to *know* His will, for how can we *do* His will if we don't *understand* His plans and desires?

───── ❖ ─────

Thankfully, we can come to know God's intentions by saturating our minds with Scripture, for His Word is His will. If we do this, our minds will be renewed.

The third and most powerful truth God tells us in this verse is that He is not going to renew our minds *for* us. Many people travel through life with the delusion that if God wants it, He will just make it happen. No, the Bible tells us *we* must renew our minds. Thinking that God is going to change your mind is as fruitless as thinking He is going to change your body. You already know that if you want to change your body, *you* have to do something constructive—like eating right and exercising, even when you don't feel so inclined.

Likewise, if you are going to see a transformation in your way of thinking, you have to put the process in motion with your own actions. You have to read your Bible, even when you'd rather be doing something else. You have to include God in your daily routine and make a quality decision to wash your mind continually with His Word.

Why do many people fail to receive what God wants them to have? Why do they fall short of becoming all the Lord desires them to be? Because they neglect to renew their minds with Scripture.

His written Word is the beginning of everything. It is our foundation, our sword—the only offensive weapon God has given us. It is there for us to wield when Satan assaults our minds with thoughts which are contrary to what God desires for us.

———— ❖ ————

When we plant His Word so it can flourish in our hearts and minds, we arm ourselves with a mighty weapon to ward off every deceptive attack of the enemy.

Then we can begin to think as God thinks and to live the abundant life He intends for us.

CLIMATE CONTROL PRINCIPLE #2
CONQUER YOUR PAST

The second climate control step you need to take in order to destroy grasshopper mentality is to *conquer your past.*

You may have seen *The Piano,* a movie that chronicles the journey toward emotional freedom of a nineteenth century single mother named Ada. Motivated by the promise of an arranged marriage, Ada moves with her young daughter from Scotland to a remote area of New Zealand. Unable to speak since childhood, Ada lives in an emotional prison of shame and anger, her sole source of pleasure being the ownership of her piano, which she had brought with her from her native land.

In New Zealand she marries a Kiwi farmer who turns out to be abusive. Then a mysterious man named George devises a plan to take her, along with her daughter and her cherished piano, away from the abusive marriage. They are to escape by sea.

But as they row away from the shore towards a waiting ship and the weight of the piano threatens to sink the dinghy, Ada suddenly gains insight into her life. She realizes that her piano has been a symbol of her shame and regret. So she signals to push the piano out of the boat.

"What did she say?" George asks the girl, Flora.

"She wants you to throw the piano overboard," Flora replies.

But convinced the piano can be saved, George counters, "It's quite safe. They are managing."

More determined, Flora speaks on her mute mother's behalf. "She says throw it overboard. She doesn't want it because it's spoiled."

Finally George gives in to Ada's request. But as the piano splashes into the sea, a rope tied to it encircles Ada's boot, and she is pulled under, sinking with the piano. She kicks and frees her foot from the boot and then frantically swims back to the surface. When her head breaks the water, she gasps her first breath as a free woman, released from the bondage of her past.[11]

Similarly, if you and I are ever going to be liberated from grasshopper mentality, we must refuse to let our negative past continue to hold us back. As God's Word tells us, *"This onething I do, forgetting those things which are behind."*[12]

We must remember to lay aside the harmful thoughts of our history and concentrate on only the positive. One way of looking at it is that *we must rewrite the script of our past.* We can't really *forget* the negative parts of what has occurred, *but we can learn from the experience.*

———— ❖ ————

We must never let yesterday tell us who we are, especially if something happened which is foreign to the victory, success and abundant life God wants us to have.

We must redefine what has taken place, just as the apostle Paul did. When we read one of the his prayers to God—*"Receive us; we have wronged no man, we have corrupted no man, we have defrauded no man ...,"*[13] we may well wonder: "Paul, what are you talking about? You murdered people. What do you mean, you have harmed no man?" But Paul gives us the answer to this objection when he later observes, "I'm a new creature in Christ Jesus. Old things are passed away; behold, all things have become new."[14]

Paul edited his earlier days. He put his own spin on prior circumstances and carried forward something which could help him develop a More Than Conqueror mentality. If he had persisted in dwelling on his past misdeeds, he could never have become an apostle of Christ.

Unlike Paul, some people develop grasshopper mentality because they still carry scars from long ago. They wear them for years, allowing their history to define who they are. From time to time problems we may not be able to prevent happen to us. But we can revise the record!

Suppose you were molested during your youth. You can't *change* what happened, but you can tell yourself, "Because *I* was abused, I'm going to be more caring and sensitive to *other* people who have experienced the same trauma. Because this happened to me, I'm going to reach out to those whom others have rejected. I am going to be a loving and supportive friend and *listener* rather than someone who is only concerned with getting his or her own point across."

In other words, you can edit or reinterpret your past by using the scars to redefine yourself today as a compassionate, loving person, a *reborn* individual with a More Than Conqueror mentality!

CONTROL PRINCIPLE # 3
PUT YOUR PRESENT IN PERSPECTIVE

Two primary characteristics of small thinking are being stuck in your past and consumed by your present. You must *put your present in perspective!*

The Israelites' response to the evil report of the ten scouts is an excellent example of grasshopper mentality's two main characteristics in action. As Numbers 14:1 tells us, *"So all the congregation lifted up their voices and cried, and the people wept that night."* We can see in their response that weeping and crying do not necessarily indicate spirituality. These people were distraught because of grasshopper mentality!

The Israelites' very next words further reveal their thinking as they reminisced fondly about their prior years in Egypt, going so far as to complain to Moses, "If only we had died in the land of Egypt!"[15]

Their words show how the Israelites were trapped in their past. And when they added a railing accusation against God, accusing Him of delivering them from Egypt only to allow them to die in the wilderness,[16] they let it be known they were also consumed by their present—and were unhappy with the way things were going!

Too often some of us resemble the Israelites as they stood at the border of the Promised Land. We become so engrossed with what is going on day by day we can't see ourselves ever moving *beyond* to better things.

———— ❖ ————

Putting our present in perspective allows us to see that what we may be experiencing is not necessarily what we must expect in the future.

In chapter four of Second Corinthians the apostle Paul tells us what this means: *We are hard pressed on every side, yet not crushed; we are perplexed, but not in despair; persecuted, but not forsaken; struck down, but not destroyed.*[17]

In effect, Paul was saying, "I'm evaluating the situation. I understand circumstances aren't going the way I want them to. I know I have problems, but I'm not going to let them control, define or condition me to believe that I must experience something far less than what God has for me. He would not allow this, and neither will I!"

Many still need to learn this lesson. They live only in the moment. Even though they may have conquered their past, they haven't learned how to climb beyond present circumstances to the next level God intends them to reach. Their lives are locked firmly in what is happening now. They struggle to hold onto what they see as their limitations, shying away from initiating change for the better. For instance, if they are currently attempting to maintain financial security, they tend to accept this battle as inevitable and one from which they can never fully escape.

If you see yourself in this picture, your destructive outlook will both frustrate and sadden the More Than Conquerors among your acquaintances who see you stuck in your past and feeling trapped in your present—a present that will ultimately become a lonely wilderness.

Because the Israelites heard and believed the ten scouts' evil report, God sent them back to the barren lands where they had wandered for forty years because they would not follow God, submit themselves to Him, and humble their hearts. In the end, nearly everyone in that generation died in the wilderness, never seeing the Promised Land.

The journey from Egypt to the land of milk and honey was supposed to be only an eleven-day venture, yet it took Israel *forty years!*[18] Moses reminded the Israelites what God had said to them during the long trek: *"The Lord our God spoke to us in Horeb, saying: 'You have dwelt long enough at this mountain.'"*[19] In effect, God's message to His people could be colloquialized as "Listen to Me, children of Israel! You've been languishing in this wilderness too long!"

It was not their enemies who kept them wandering in the desert, nor was it the trials they experienced along the way. The blame can be attributed to their grasshopper mentality.

———— ❖ ————

We need to understand that the enemy can't exercise his power over our lives unless we give him permission.

But it usually isn't the devil, other people, or the circumstances which keep us confined to the wilderness. It is our own thinking!

Pessimistic people tend to wait for someone else to help them reach their Promised Land or for an extraordinary event to magically change things for the better. They resemble the paralyzed man at the pool of Bethesda in John's gospel who, when Jesus asked him if he wanted to be made well, replied,

"But I don't have any man to help me."[20] Like this invalid, grasshoppers are always waiting for their big break. More Than Conquerors, on the other hand, create their own destiny. They don't wait for the stars, the moon and the sun to all come into alignment. They don't settle for basking in the memory of past accomplishments. Overcomers move ahead to make great things happen!

Caleb was an overcomer. He told the children of Israel to stop wallowing in doubt and unbelief and let their faith motivate them to do what God had told them.[21] Faith must be translated into action in order to bring to pass what God wants for His children.

Scripture declares that faith without works is dead.[22] Believing by itself is not enough, because to be effective, belief must go hand in hand with action. Faith requires us to believe in God and His Word even in the absence of material or physical proof, but we must *act* on our faith to make it work for us and lead us to our Promised Land.

If we are thirsty and there is a glass of water sitting on the table in front of us, our thirst will never be quenched unless we pick up the glass and drink the water. Likewise, the only way we can become satisfied and nourished both spiritually and materially by the Promised Feast God has set before us, is to reach out actively and partake.

TAKE A SPIRITUAL "TIMEOUT"

Putting our present in perspective requires a spiritual pause, like the timeout a good basketball coach calls for when his team, which has been in the lead, suddenly falls behind. The reason for this is that the coach needs to put the game in perspective for his players. He encourages them, "Hey, guys, we're only down a point, and we have fifteen minutes left in the game. The fact they've taken the lead doesn't mean we're going to lose. We just need to bear down and go back to the kind of playing that gave us the lead up to this point."

The way to take a *spiritual* timeout is by meditating on God's promises as they apply to you personally. Concentrate on seeing yourself as the *Lord* sees you according to His Word. The approach involves controlling the nature of what we see, hear and say. And a good time to think on His promises is when things are going badly. Praying quashes anxiety, worry, and vain imaginings and replaces them with the positive power of hope and divine perspective.

God's wish was that the Israelites would travel eleven days through the wilderness—straight into the Promised Land. But because of grasshopper mentality, they wandered forty years, most of them dying along the way without reaching their destination.

————— ❖ —————

The Lord wants all of us to live full and fruitful lives in our personal Promised Lands, but we can only translate our faith in God's promise into reality by doing our part.

As the old saying goes, "God helps those who help themselves." And the way we can do this is to abandon negative thinking in favor of a More Than Conqueror mentality and meditate positively on what lies ahead, exercising control over what we see, hear and say.

My reaction to a recent personal emergency might serve to illustrate this point. My wife phoned me at my office to beg me to come right home because my son Joey, whom I could hear crying in the background, had somehow got a dangerous substance in one of his eyes.

All the way home I leaned on my faith to assure me God would make things right and that Joey was going to be fine. Because I had trust in my heavenly Father, my meditation was on *Him*. So I wasn't tempted to doubt or be consumed by anxiety. I *knew* no harm to my family or to me could prevail.

And, as it always is, my faith was justified by the outcome. After we spent only a few minutes cleansing his eye by flushing it with water, Joey was just fine.

PERCEPTION IS REALITY

We are told in Deuteronomy how Moses reminded the Israelites that the Lord had blessed them as much as He could, even when they suffered from fearful thoughts:

> *So he humbled you, allowed you to hunger, and fed you with manna which you did not know nor did your fathers know, that he might make you know that man shall not live by bread alone; but man lives by every word that proceeds from the mouth of the Lord. Your garments did not wear out on you, nor did your foot swell these forty years.*[23]

What a miracle! Imagine walking in the desert for that long without suffering from swollen feet! It was as if God were saying, "Even with your poor attitude, I will still bless you. I will still care for you and provide your daily bread."

God wants us to see His goodness so we can begin to focus our thinking on His promised benefits rather than on the often negative aspects of our lives. The way we think is essential to the achievement of what God intends for us. It determines who we are, where and how far we will go. *Perception is reality.* What you believe about yourself or your circumstances will determine the reality you experience in life.

I recently read a story about a family who purchased an old farm at a time when rural water lines were just being developed. The farm was at the very end of the water line, and the previous owners told the family who purchased the farm that the water pressure was consistently low.

So the new owners tolerated the bad water pressure for two years, thinking it was just an irritation they had to live with. Consequently, they were astonished one morning when they opened a tap and, instead of the expected trickle, a rushing torrent of water poured out. But rather than trying to determine what had caused the sudden improvement, they just accepted their good fortune until about a month later when the water pressure once more reverted back to a trickle.

At this point they phoned the water company for an explanation and were told that being at the end of the water line had nothing to do with the poor pressure. The problem was a faulty pump, which had finally been replaced. The new pump had just developed a problem, but it would soon be taken care of and the water pressure restored.

The family had unnecessarily lived with this situation for two years because they had perceived as truth that the low water pressure was caused by their being at the end of the water line. Calling the water company to inquire about the problem didn't occur to them. If they had bothered to check it out, they could have had good water pressure from the beginning!

Perception *determines* the experience we will have. Consequently, *faulty* thinking will cause us to live far below our potential. Many of us have far less than what God wants us to have because we allow an inaccurate perception to be our reality. All that is needed to redirect our lives is to replace the wrong view with the truth of who we are in God— More Than Conquerors through Him who loves us!

Much in life may be negotiable, but perceptions are not. So we must not believe the lie that we are average, ordinary and unable to overcome the challenges we face in life. Call on your God! Seek out His promises and find out what He has to say concerning you and your potential. Accurately perceiving your life is directly dependent on welcoming God's message into your heart.

Many people come to church and hear the Word, but are blocked from the light it should inspire because they arrive with a closed mind and spirit. Most of the service can pass before they finally break through the worldly barriers and actually receive anything from the Lord. The Bible never tells us that God's Word in and of itself will change the light in which we walk. Instead we are told that "the *entrance* of God's words gives light; they give understanding to the simple."[24] Scripture changes the way you think and the way you perceive the situations you face, however, only when it enters your inner man.

───────── ❖ ─────────

If you come into the Father's presence with an open spirit, the entrance of His Word will give you light and help you clearly see yourself.

The problem with all of the scouts except for Caleb and Joshua was their perception was flawed. Each of them heard God's promise: *"The land you are going to possess is yours, for I have given it to you. Every place that the sole of your foot shall tread upon shall be yours."*[25] Of the thousands who heard this divine promise from Heaven, only two took it into their hearts. Except for Caleb and Joshua, the scouts didn't understand who God was and what He was like. Maybe the outcome would have been different if they had known *"Every good gift and every perfect gift is from above, and cometh down from the Father of lights, with whom is no variableness, neither shadow of turning"*[26] Perhaps then they would have understood that God had given them the Promised Land, giants or no giants!

But the ten scouts who returned with negative reports didn't perceive God correctly, so they did not know He never promises what He cannot perform. Also, because they failed to have a proper perception of their supposed enemy, they didn't understand that the Almighty was bigger and more powerful than the giants. They were wrong to think the enemy was stronger than they were, because no foe can defeat God's people when they act in faith.

The other children of Israel suffered with the same perception problem. They saw the ten scouts as a more reliable source of truth than God Himself and gave more credence to their report than to the Lord's promise.

───────── ❖ ─────────

Unfortunately, we too are often tempted to put more stock in what we see than in the truth of God's Word.

Finally, and perhaps most important, the ten scouts didn't have a proper perception of *themselves*. They thought they were "as grasshoppers in our enemies' sight"— probably reasoning that if only God had given them a land inhabited by weak and helpless people, maybe then they could have recommended entering the Promised Land. But they believed there was no way they could defeat those giants.

Too many people feel the same way instead of perceiving themselves as God sees them, thereby allowing His divine Word to enter and fill them with light.

When we accept the Lord's plan we will develop an entirely different outlook from that of grasshoppers who fail to take these steps. He will give us a divinely inspired perception which changes the way we see ourselves. When we look in the mirror, we will see a righteous child of God, filled with His glory and with the power to think like a More Than Conqueror, no matter what challenges we face.

CHAPTER THREE

THINKING LIKE A MORE THAN CONQUEROR

Although two of the twelve scouts, Joshua and Caleb, understood the integrity of God's promise and trusted that no matter what they might encounter, He intended victory for them, when the other ten returned from their reconnaissance in the Promised Land with a bad report, all of the Israelites were swayed by it. As a result, most of the children of Israel were never able to enter their Promised Land.

Just as He had a plan for the Israelites, God has a plan that will lead to victory in all of our lives—if we can conquer grasshopper mentality and hold to our faith in His promise rather than allow ourselves to be distracted by our fear of transient circumstances.

WILLINGNESS TO STAND OUT FROM THE CROWD

All of the twelve scouts were under the same leadership, had witnessed the same miracles, had seen the same giants, had tasted the same grapes, and had been given the same promise; but only two of them chose to stand out from the crowd by holding onto their faith and recommending *taking* their Promised Land.

God wants us to understand there will always be more

grasshoppers than those in the More Than Conquerors category. In this case the ratio was five to one.

Grasshoppers blend in because they are all just alike. They don't make waves or cause others to feel uncomfortable by *challenging* them.

However, God doesn't want us to be just *conquerors*, although this would be excellent. He desires for us to be *More Than Conquerors!*[1] But if you are going to be overcomers, you will have to accustom yourself to not being part of the in-crowd. Many fall short in their relationship with God because they lack the courage to stand up against what others tell them they ought to be doing instead of putting their faith in what *God* wants them to accomplish.

---- ❖ ----

The Lord desires for us to be eagles with the courage to fly alone rather than in flocks, as other birds do.

Choosing the comfortable path and following the crowd will get us nowhere in life; but when we choose to live as More Than Conquerors, we set ourselves on individual paths to our own *personal* destinies—the fulfillment of a divine purpose that is uniquely our own. The option is between popularity or triumph over mediocrity. God doesn't want us to be motivated by a desire for popularity; rather to overcome "average" and soar like eagles! Since *God* has what we need, we have to remain focused and sometimes have the courage to stand alone.

Of course, our heavenly Father doesn't require or expect us to be isolationists. We need to avoid those whose influence would lead us astray, but at the same time we should welcome the help of individuals who will stand behind us as we seek to achieve what God tells us to do with our lives. And instead of pursuing the accolades of others, we must yearn to hear the *Master*'s praise: "Well done, good and faithful servant."[2] We should not be concerned with what people might say if we ignore them to obey God. When this, rather than the approval of men, is our goal, the Lord will eventually exalt us and make our names great.[3] He has a way of making us popular, even when we see the need to take an unpopular stand.

A story about a little-known senator from Kansas illustrates the power of and reward for being willing to stand alone. U.S. Senator Edmund G. Ross of Kansas might be thought of as a "Mr. Nobody." No law bears his name. Not a single list of Senate "greats" mentions his service. But although when Ross entered the Senate in 1866, he was considered the man to watch, he tossed it all away by one courageous act of conscience.

Conflict was dividing our government in the wake of the Civil War. President Andrew Johnson was determined to follow Lincoln's policy of reconciliation toward the defeated South, but Congress seemed equally determined to rule the defeated Confederate states with an iron hand.

Congress decided to strike first. Shortly after Senator Ross was seated, the Senate introduced impeachment proceedings against the hated President. The radicals calculated that they needed thirty-six votes, and smiled as they concluded that the thirty-sixth was none other than Ross. The new senator listened to the vigilante talk. Yet, to the surprise of many, he declared that the President "deserved as fair a trial as any accused man has ever had on earth." But when word went out that his vote was "shaky," Ross received an avalanche of anti-Johnson telegrams from every section of the country, and radical senators badgered him to "come to his senses."

When the fateful voting day arrived, tickets for admission

were at an enormous premium and the Senate galleries were packed.

A deathlike stillness fell over the Senate chamber as the oral vote reached Ross. With twenty-eight "guilty" votes already recorded and eleven more "guilties" assured, only Ross's vote was needed to impeach the President.

Unable to conceal his emotion, the Chief Justice asked in a trembling voice, "Mr. Senator Ross, how vote you? Is the respondent Andrew Johnson guilty as charged?"

Ross's response was strong and unhesitating: "Not guilty!" Senator Ross had decided to *stand alone*, and with his dissenting vote, the trial was over.

The public's response was as predicted. A high official from Kansas wired Ross to chastise him: "Kansas repudiates you as she does all perjurers and skunks."

Ross later explained that at the moment he announced his vote, he had looked into his open grave. "Friendships, position, fortune, and everything that makes life desirable to an ambitious man were about to be swept away by the breath of my mouth, perhaps forever."

And the "open grave" vision became a reality. Ross's political career lay in ruins. Extreme ostracism and even physical attack awaited his family upon their return home. But Ross remained confident of the wisdom of his decision, telling his wife, "Millions cursing me today will bless me tomorrow, though only God can know the struggle it has cost me."

It was a prophetic declaration. Twenty years later Congress and the Supreme Court officially affirmed the wisdom of Ross's position by changing the rules of impeachment. Ross was appointed Territorial Governor of New Mexico and just before his death was awarded a special pension by Congress. The press and country followed by honoring his courage, which, they finally conceded, had saved their nation from a divisive crisis. Senator Ross had been willing to stand out from the crowd even at the cost of an extremely high personal price. At a crucial moment, though, God had enabled a More Than Conqueror to soar like an eagle![4]

EQUIPPED WITH DIVINE PURPOSE

As has already been noted, God is not the cause of negative things or conditions, but rather only the source of "every good and every perfect gift."[5] Nor does God discriminate because of birth, upbringing, or education. So since the Lord wants and expects the best for all of us, there must be a different reason why some people achieve whereas others fail. The reason is that in addition to being willing to stand alone, More Than Conquerors need to commit themselves to the purpose for which God created them.

Reflect back on those twelve scouts in Numbers 13. They had been chosen because they were the finest and best-equipped leaders of their various tribes, yet only two of them returned from reconnoitering with a report that would have led to a quick entrance into the Promised Land if only the Israelites hadn't let themselves be swayed by the negative report of the other ten. The essential difference between Caleb and Joshua and the others, who were grasshoppers, was that they never allowed fear or misgivings to divert them. They never doubted that God would help them to triumph, whereas the ten grasshoppers let their dread of worldly giants move them to ignore or abandon the divine purpose set before them.

---❖---

As was true with Caleb and Joshua, it is purpose that propels us all forward when others turn aside.

Seeing how vital it is to know and embrace one's purpose, we must ask ourselves what purpose *is*.

- It is the end for which the means exists.
- It is a desired result that initiates production.
- It is the need that causes a manufacturer to produce a specific product.
- It is the destination that prompts the journey.
- It is the objective for the subject.
- It is the aspiration for the inspiration.
- It is the goal that one resolves to pursue and possess.

Ultimately, purpose is the original intent in the mind of the Creator that motivated Him to create a particular item, thing, or person.[6]

GIANTS: STOP SIGNS OR SIGNPOSTS?

Numbers 13 provides three proofs that having a divinely inspired purpose, or not having one, was the primary difference between the ten grasshoppers and the two More Than Conquerors: their reaction to the giants, their speech, and their focus.

Let's first look at their respective reaction to the giants. People who understand and follow through on the purpose God intends for them don't see giants the same way that people without such a purpose see them. Those who don't understand or act in accordance with their purpose view giants as Stop Signs. To them, giants impose insurmountable odds—obstacles that are too big to overcome. They either retreat or remain trapped in the box they are already in when they encounter giants. At best, purposeless people see their status as the best life has to offer.

———— ❖ ————

Individuals who understand and are motivated by the purpose God intends for them, see giants as no more than temporary obstacles at the border of their Promised Land that God will help them to overcome.

They know there is nothing to be afraid of because the Lord is with them, and they even see challenges as evidence that the Almighty has gone before them, leaving only those obstacles He knows they are able to conquer with the power He has instilled in them.

The episode in the film *The Wizard of Oz* in which Dorothy, the Scarecrow, the Tin Man, and the Cowardly Lion travel to the Emerald City to ask the help of the mighty Wizard could well serve as a parable about reacting to giants we encounter on our path to purpose fulfillment.

When they finally reach the wizard's castle, they enter a huge room, where they hear the frighteningly loud, deep voice of the Wizard but see only the scary image of a big, stern face on the wall. The four begin to shake in fear, with the terrified Cowardly Lion even jumping up into the Scarecrow's arms when the Wizard's booming voice echoes throughout the hall.

But then the little dog Toto runs over to a nearby curtain, grabs hold of it with his teeth, and pulls it down. Behind the curtain, the intimidating Wizard turns out to be nothing more than a little old man using a voice machine! And courage quickly returns to the four astonished companions when they realize that the horrifying "giant" was only a trick intended to frighten them away.

This is what those who know their purpose eventually find out. The giants we encounter in life usually have a much greater bark than bite!

David understood that although giants may be fearful to see and hear, they are really no match for anyone motivated and empowered by a God-given purpose. As a result, the teenage shepherd boy defeated Goliath with only a slingshot and a few stones.[7]

---------- ❖ ----------

When you encounter a giant on your path to victory, don't think of it as a Stop Sign, but rather a Sign Post pointing to your destiny!

PURPOSE AFFECTS OUR SPEECH— THE THOUGHTS WE PUT INTO WORDS

The second proof in Numbers 13 that the presence or absence of God-inspired *purpose* was the primary difference between the grasshoppers and the More Than Conquerors can be seen in the contrasting thoughts expressed in their *speech*. The grasshoppers said "We're not able to go up against the people, for they are stronger than we," whereas the More Than Conquerors proclaimed "Let's go up at once and possess it, for we are well able to overcome the giants!"

Grasshopper conversations often includes phrases such as "*I can't do that because...*" "*It's not possible,*" "*I don't have...*" "*I can't afford to do that,*" *Well, that's just life,*" and "*I'm really not good at that sort of thing.*" Remember, inferior mentality is characterized by a small, insignificant view of oneself. Thinking they must appear outwardly humble, grasshoppers belittle themselves. But as noted earlier, they misunderstand the nature of true humility—that real humility is a position in respect to God, not an appearance before others. When we try to prove we're humble, we succeed only in proving that we are not!

Another grasshopper giveaway is that they are consistently unwilling to say what they believe God will do or accomplish. "God is *able*," they will say, "but we can never know what He will do." Or they will hedge by commenting, "God can cure you of that sickness" instead of committing themselves by confidently asserting, "God *will* cure you of that sickness."

Saying the Almighty *can* do something instead of boldly committing oneself in the knowledge that He *will do what is positive and good* is the vocabulary of a grasshopper. It's all right to boldly declare God's goodness, for He himself has declared, *"For I know the thoughts that I think toward you, says the Lord, thoughts of peace and not of evil, to give you a future and a hope."*[8] But grasshoppers lack the courage to speak this boldly. They show themselves to be more concerned about the opinion others might have of them if things don't go the way they planned.

More Than Conquerors are quite a different breed—their speech consistently affirming their faith with phrases such as "I can do all things through Christ, who strengthens me," "With God nothing is impossible," "That difficult situation will surely change," and, most revealing, "I may not know yet how I'm going to solve this problem, but God has said if I ask Him, He will give me the wisdom and strength to succeed. So I know that I can do it!"

I can think of no more graphic illustration of how the power of our words inspires a "can do" attitude than the classic children's story "The Little Engine That Could."

A little steam engine was doing very well until she came to a steep hill. But then, no matter how hard she tried, she couldn't move the long train of cars she was pulling. She tried and she tried. She puffed and she puffed. But the cars just wouldn't go up the hill.

Finally, refusing to give up, she left the load she had been trying to pull and started up the track, looking for someone to help her. When she came alongside a big steam engine that looked very strong standing on a sidetrack, she ran alongside and asked him, "Will you help me over the hill with my train of cars? It is so long and heavy that I can't get it over by myself."

But the big steam engine's response was, "Don't you see that I am through with my day's work? I have been rubbed and scoured ready for my next run. No, I cannot help you."

Still refusing to give up, the little engine went on until she came to another big engine. But this one too turned her down, telling her that he had been working very hard and was too tired to help.

So, sad but still determined, she went on until after awhile she came to a little steam engine just like herself. "Will you help me over the hill with my train of cars?" she asked."

"Yes, indeed!" replied the little steam engine. "I'll be glad to help you, if I can."

And together the two little engines went to where the train of cars had been standing, and one behind the other at the head of the train, off they went, slowly climbing the steep hill and singing together, "I think I can, I think I can, I think I can."

And they did! Very soon they were over the hill, going down the other side, and finally on the plain again, where the first little engine, after saying goodbye to her helpful friend, went happily on her way, singing, "I thought I could, I thought I could, I thought I could![9]

So, like the Little Engine That Could, don't allow yourself to sing the song of grasshoppers that complains "I can't." Begin releasing your faith by confidently repeating "I can," and you will be able to reach and enter your personal Promised Land.

FOCUS ON THE <u>PROMISE</u>, NOT ON THE <u>PROBLEM</u>

The third proof in Numbers 13 indicating that purpose is the primary difference between grasshoppers and More Than Conquerors is the contrast in *focus* of the two groups. People with God-directed purpose are centered on the promise, not on the problem, whereas people without purpose look at the problem, not the promise.

The focus of the unnamed ten scouts with grasshopper mentality was on the giants, while Joshua and Caleb saw the grapes. The giants were the *problem*; the grapes symbolized the *promise*.

Neither Joshua nor Caleb denied or ignored the existence of giants, but they were motivated by their faith in the truth of God's promise and were able to zero in on the grapes.

Similarly, if we are ill or have another condition, we needn't *deny* the illness or problem; we need to claim the assurance of a cure or solution we can achieve by remembering that through His suffering and sacrifice, Jesus bore *our* pain. In the same way that the Lord conquered the giants for us long ago, we can be assured of triumph over them if we look beyond their shadow and keep our attention on the grapes.

---------- ❖ ----------

We need to avoid being problem-conscious in favor of being God-conscious—and learn to weigh our grapes instead of measuring our giants.

God had said, "I've given you the land. It's yours. The fruit there is blessed, for it is a land that flows with milk and honey." Joshua and Caleb wouldn't let go of the promise, no matter how many giants they saw along the way. While these two More Than Conquerors were scouting the land, they remained centered on God's promise. They not only meditated on the Lord's pledge; they carried it back to the Israelite camp in the form of the huge cluster of grapes.

Joshua and Caleb had spent much time contemplating God's assurance by the time they returned to the camp. And just as a dedication to God's promises always does, Joshua and Caleb's resulting faith led them to embrace its truth with conviction.

You too will find your answer if you meditate and remain focused on what God has said. The Lord emphasized this key to success when He told Joshua, *"This Book of the Law shall not depart from your mouth, but you shall meditate in it day and night, that you may observe to do according to all that is written in it. For then you will make your way prosperous, and then you will have good success."*[10]

God was telling Joshua to spend time *dwelling* on His promise so he could *visualize* the answer.

———— ❖ ————

The purpose of meditation is to lead us to envision the answer or solution we seek, because we need to be able to see something—to have an inner vision—before we can fully accept and effectively act on it.

And one of the most valuable and precious gifts God has given us is our ability to envision through prayer.

JESUS KNEW HIS PURPOSE
No one else has ever surpassed Jesus in the ability to speak

like a More Than Conqueror. He knew He had come to this earth for a specific purpose—*"that he might destroy the works of the Devil."*[11] And Jesus spoke accordingly. Once, He even stood before the tomb of His good friend Lazarus and summoned the man to arise saying, "Lazarus come forth," and Lazarus did![12] Now that's knowing your purpose and speaking with authority!

Notice the confidence with which Jesus spoke. He didn't cringe in humility with words like "O God, if it be thy will, please, etc. etc." He didn't try, with self-effacing humility, to conceal His personal relationship with God from those who stood around Him; nor did He hesitate to speak with conviction and power.

Those present marveled at His directness and confidence: *"What a word this is! For with authority and power he commands the unclean spirits, and they come out!"*[13] Jesus knew His reason for coming to earth, and He spoke with purpose-inspired speech.

And at the end of His ministry, when He had been betrayed and stood before Pontius Pilate, who asked Him if He was a king, His unhesitating response was, *"You say rightly that I am a king. For this cause I was born and for this cause I have come into the world, that I should bear witness to the truth. Everyone who is of the truth hears my voice."*[14]

Jesus was telling him, "I was born for a reason. I came to earth for a purpose, and this is the only thing I am focused on." Jesus knew His calling, and consequently His speech was that of a winner. And to be like Him, we must find our purpose as well.

FROM GRASSHOPPER TO OVERCOMER
This is probably a good time for you to decide whether you

qualify as a More Than Conqueror or whether you still suffer from grasshopper mentality.

Fortunately, if you're still undecided there is good news. God is proficient at turning grasshoppers into More Than Conquerors. He did it for Moses, and He can surely do it for you!

One day God spoke to Moses from a burning bush, saying, *"Come now, therefore, and I will send you to Pharaoh, that you may bring my people, the children of Israel out of Egypt. "*[15] By telling this to Moses, God gave him his purpose.

Then Moses confessed to the Almighty, *"O my Lord, I am not eloquent, neither heretofore nor since you have spoken to your servant: but I am slow of speech and slow of tongue."*[16]

Some might assume that God ought to have been favorably impressed by this response, reasoning that Moses was showing himself to be appropriately humble. After all, the Bible says that Moses was the meekest and most humble man who ever lived, although he was the one to write this about himself.

So the Lord asked him, *"Who has made man's mouth? Or who makes the mute, the deaf, the seeing, or the blind? Have not I, the Lord? Now therefore go, and I will be with your mouth and teach you what you will say."*[17] In effect, God was telling Moses, "Shape up! I created you! Surely you ought to realize I put into you all of the abilities and skills you need to succeed!"

In spite of his protests, Moses really didn't have a speech problem. The Bible tells us he was educated in all the ways of the Egyptians and that he was both very intelligent and well spoken. However, when God gave him his marching orders, he acted like a grasshopper. Even after God had assured him he was well qualified for the job, Moses begged, *"O Lord, please send someone else to do it."*[18]

Instead of pleasing God, Moses' persistent self effacement

both displeased and angered Him.[19] Mercifully, though, God showed Moses His power and His ability to do all things. The Lord told Moses to throw down his staff, and when he obeyed, the staff turned into a serpent. Then God instructed him to pick up the serpent, and it turned back into a staff again. The Lord said to Moses, "Stick your hand in your coat," and Moses obeyed. Then he pulled it out again, and his hand was leprous. When God told him to do it once more, Moses' hand became whole again.[20]

Moses ultimately overcame his misgivings and developed a More Than Conqueror mentality. Afterward, he and Aaron went in and told Pharaoh, *"Thus says the Lord God of Israel: 'Let my people go that they may hold a feast to me in the wilderness!'"*[21] With God's help, Moses eventually accepted and became comfortable with his purpose and was functioning as a deliverer of his people.

God is similarly displeased and angered when we see ourselves or act like grasshoppers. But we can learn from the example above that our God is unshakable in His willingness and intent to guide and keep us on the path He has set for us.

YOU ARE GOD'S MASTERPIECE

You will have to understand how to think like a More Than Conqueror before you can become one. First of all, *you must believe in yourself.*

---------- ❖ ----------

We sometimes make the mistake of thinking we are to believe only in God rather than confidently have faith in ourselves.

It is certainly true that we must have confidence in God,

knowing He will do what He has promised, that He is the Source of everything good in our lives, that He is our Answer, and that He is the One we need in time of trouble.

This belief is paramount. We also need to believe in ourselves. Remember, God Himself declares we are His masterpieces,[22] fearfully and wonderfully made![23] And since God is our architect, we owe it to Him to believe in ourselves. When we do, we unlock the potential the Creator has built into each of us.

Roger Bannister believed in himself, and you may recall how he permanently changed the landscape of track and field. For years people had believed that running a mile in less than four minutes was humanly impossible. Then, in 1954, Bannister proved everyone had been wrong.

Roger was a medical student who decided to take up running as a hobby. Shortly thereafter, he became determined to break the seemingly insurmountable four-minute mile barrier in spite of the fact that everyone told him such a dream was an impossible one. Even the doctors in medical school told him that breaking the four-minute mile couldn't be done, cautioning him that "a man's heart would explode" if he ran that fast.

But believing in himself and thinking that he *could* when others tried to persuade him that he *couldn't*, Roger refused to be dissuaded. He even had a special pair of expensive lightweight leather shoes made to help him attain his goal, in spite of the fact, as he told a friend, that he felt guilty about spending so much money on something he would be using for less than four minutes.

And sure enough, Roger *did* it, setting what was then the world record and giving many other runners hope. Within one year, thirty-seven other runners broke that belief barrier. The year after, another 300 did the same thing.[24]

How did Roger achieve his goal? He believed in himself.

When the ten unnamed scouts said "We are grasshoppers," they betrayed their lack of belief not only in themselves, but in the Lord as well. Their speech gave them away. They didn't believe God's power working through them was enough to make it possible to take the land.

We need to realize how much the Lord is saddened when we make this same mistake.

❖

Since we are His creations, we actually <u>offend</u> the Father when we fail to believe in ourselves!

In the book of Psalms, David praised God for making him the sort of person he believed himself to be: *"I will praise you, for I am fearfully and wonderfully made; marvelous are your works; and that my soul knows very well."*[25] David knew what it meant to be God's creation, and in response, the Lord called David *a man after his own heart.*

Since, like David, you too are a work of Almighty God; and because His works are perfect, this means you are a *masterpiece*, the highest form of His creation. If you fail to see yourself this way, you need to revise your thinking. Start believing in yourself and in your ability to reach your Promised Land!

EXPECT VICTORY AND SUCCESS

Believing in ourselves encourages us to expect victory and success. It also makes it possible for us to concentrate on objectives, confront and overcome problems and obstacles, and triumph. Instead of allowing ourselves to be intimidated by the frightening giants, we automatically focus on the bounty of the land—on success and victory.

A minister whom I once heard speak on the subject imaginatively illustrated the point this way: Your mind is like a busy thought factory producing countless thoughts every day. Production in this factory is under the authority of two foremen, Mr. Triumph and Mr. Defeat. Mr. Triumph is in charge of manufacturing positive thoughts, such as *I can be victorious* and *I can do all things through Christ, who strengthens me.* He specializes in reasons why you can, why you're qualified, and why you *will* enjoy your Promised Land. The other foreman, Mr. Defeat, produces negative, depressing thoughts. He's the expert on developing reasons why you *can't.* His specialty is convincing you that you're going to fail.

Both Mr. Triumph and Mr. Defeat are intensely responsive. The moment you signal him or give him evidence of the slightest mental inclination, each foreman immediately snaps to attention and is at your beck and call.

If the signal is positive, Mr. Triumph steps forward and begins to go to work. On the other hand, if you dwell on negative thoughts, Mr. Defeat steps forward. And the more work you give either foreman, the stronger he becomes.

If you give Mr. Defeat more work, he adds personnel and begins to take over, consuming the entire thought manufacturing process. At this point, virtually everything you think about is set on proving why you *can't* do something. As a result, you begin to think of yourself as a grasshopper.

The only intelligent response if this happens is to fire Mr. Defeat. Realize that he certainly won't help you get to where God wants to take you.

You'll never enter your Promised Land in Mr. Defeat's company. In fact, if you allow him to stay active in your thought factory, he will eventually destroy you.

This is why you should depend on Mr. Triumph one hundred percent of the time. When a thought enters your mind, ask him to begin his work.

❖

When a problem or objective is before you,
immediately begin to think positive thoughts
in keeping with the Word of God.

Which of the thought factory foremen you depend on has everything to do with the way you perceive yourself. When you view yourself as insignificant, Mr. Defeat always steps forward. When you see yourself as a God-created masterpiece, Mr. Triumph automatically takes over and begins to empower you with spiritual strength.

We allow Mr. Triumph to control our lives by feeding him the right thoughts. So condition yourself to dwell on life-enhancing images that strengthen your belief in yourself. Don't allow negative thoughts to cause you to miss your Promised Land.[26]

FIND A CURE FOR "EXCUSE-ITIS"

The second step towards thinking like a More Than Conqueror is to *cure yourself of excuse-itis*, the failure disease.

We saw that even Moses had this condition when the Lord spoke to him out of the burning bush and commanded him to go before Pharaoh and tell him to let His people go. Moses tried to avoid accepting God's assignment with an excuse about his inadequacy for the job, complaining he wasn't eloquent enough.[27]

But in effect God's reaction was to come back with, "I won't accept excuses, Moses. You need to go and do what I told you to do. Don't try to beg off by claiming you are slow of speech or that you lack eloquence! I expect you to see yourself as My masterpiece, a work of My hand."

God desires for us to rid ourselves of excuse-itis, a mind-deadening disease associated with grasshopper mentality. The Lord never utilizes people afflicted with this condition because it renders them useless.

The more successful we are, the less inclined we are to make excuses. People with mediocre accomplishments are quick to explain *why they are not, why they don't have,* and *why they can't* do this or that, but successful people realize how excuses serve only to block one's path toward achievement.

Franklin Roosevelt could have used his wealth and lifeless legs as an excuse for living an idle life. Harry Truman could have used his lack of a college education as an excuse to remain a haberdasher instead of serving his country politically. And Lyndon Johnson and Dwight Eisenhower could have used their heart attacks as excuses for retreating from public office. All of them could have succumbed to excuse-itis, but they each refused to allow themselves to be debilitated by this disease.

MANAGE YOUR ENVIRONMENT

A third characteristic of More Than Conquerors is that they *manage their environment.* The book of Romans counsels us: *"And do not be conformed to this world, but be transformed by the renewing of your mind."*[28] God is telling us if *we* don't manage our environment, it will manage *us!*

To be *"conformed" to the world* means *to have one's mind and character fashioned by the world.* Just as the body becomes what the body is fed, so the mind becomes what it is fed. Unlike food for the body which comes in neat packages purchased at the local supermarket, mind food consists of all the world's countless voices. And it is these worldly voices which cause both our conscious and subconscious thought patterns to be what they are.

———— ❖ ————

So the size of our thinking, our goals, our attitudes, and the very personality we possess are all largely shaped by our environment, the external things by which we allow ourselves to be influenced.

If we want to become More Than Conquerors, therefore, we need to manage the arena in which we live.

The first rule to follow is *making God the biggest part of your environment.* Spend time daily with Him. Study His Word. Seek His fellowship. Sit in His presence and commune with Him. Don't just go to God and tell Him what you need or want; find out what He is like and what He desires.

Another important way to keep God in your environment is to attend church regularly.

Some people look for every excuse possible to miss church. They rationalize, "I give God ten months of the year, but in the summertime, weekends are mine to go out on my boat!" Or if they think they have a cold coming on, they use it as an excuse for staying home.

People who think like this are grasshoppers! They are also the first ones who wonder why nothing good is happening in their lives. The main reason, of course, is that God isn't the most important factor in their existence.

The second rule is *to make your environment work for you, not against you.* Don't let negative influences weaken or hinder your faith. And do not associate with "you-can't-do-it" people whose pronouncements and advice promote doubt and defeat. I call such individuals "basement people," because they are always dragging others down.

It reminds me of the barber who continually expressed a negative attitude. Every time one particular customer went to have a haircut, the barber would complain and project such negativity that the customer would always leave depressed. But on one occasion the man managed to resist the barber's gloomy influence.

"I'm going to Italy," he enthusiastically told the barber. "It's going to be a very exciting trip. I have always wanted to go there."

Typically, the barber countered with remarks on how overrated Italian hotels were, how generally poor and overpriced the restaurants were, and how consistently rude Italians were to Americans, assuring the customer that he was in for a miserable experience.

But the upbeat customer resisted the negative barrage. "No, it's going to be wonderful. I'll be staying at a great hotel, eating in fabulous restaurants, and I am even going to get to see the Pope."

Predictably, the barber retorted with "That's not going to happen. He's too busy. You will never see him."

But off to Italy went the customer; and on his next trip to the barber after his return, he raved enthusiastically, "It was wonderful! I stayed in a fabulous place, ate sumptuous food, and found the Italian people absolutely delightful to be around. And I even got to see the Pope! I was going through the line, and he called me over and granted me a private audience, where I knelt down and kissed the Pope's ring when he held it out!"

For once the barber was actually impressed.

"What did the Pope say to you?" the barber excitedly asked.

"He asked me who gave me the lousy haircut!" the customer replied.

We must not allow others to drag us down. If our environment is going to work for us and not against us, we must decide to disassociate with basement people and start associating with balcony people instead.

Third, *don't let small-thinking people hold you back.* Those who are envious of you, for instance, either consciously or unconsciously *want* you to fail because your successes make them uncomfortably aware of their own shortcomings. You must not give such people the satisfaction of watching you give up in defeat.

❖

Keep your eye on the prize and remain determined to possess your Promised Land.

Fourth, *look to successful people for advice.* Many seem to enjoy giving their opinion, even when no one has asked them for it; but you should avoid listening to such "free-lance counselors." Bear in mind that ten out of every twelve people are grasshoppers whose words should not be welcomed by anyone seeking to become a More Than Conqueror.

Finally, *cast "thought poison" such as gossip and negative reports out of your environment,* even if the source is people who are close to you. God has placed us here on earth for a limited time to fulfill a purpose during our lifetime, and we can't allow "thought poison" spread by others to infect our minds.

PURPOSE: THE KEY TO THINKING LIKE A MORE THAN CONQUEROR

Ultimately, the single most determining factor in

conditioning ourselves to think like More Than Conquerors is to *know our purpose*. We spoke about that earlier, I want to further explore the topic.

Remember, purpose "is the original intent in the mind of the Creator which motivated Him to create a particular item."[29] It is the reason we are here on earth for our allotted time. It was the original intent in the mind of God which motivated Him to make you and me.

God underscores the importance of purpose when He tells fathers: *"Like arrows in the hand of a warrior, so are the children of one's youth."*[30] God is saying, "Listen, fathers, you are called to point your children in the direction of their purpose, just as an archer aims his arrow at a desired target."

A Bible story replete with evidence of the significance of purpose is the account of the conflict between David and Goliath.

Most of us are familiar with the battle scene in the story; but it is the events that lead up to the conflict which reveal how David's victory was inspired by the awareness of his purpose.

———— ❖ ————

Just days before David stepped onto the battlefield to face Goliath, he discovered that God's purpose for him was to be Israel's next king.

God instructed Samuel the prophet to go to the house of Jesse, David's father, to choose Israel's next king from among Jesse's sons. So Samuel went and announced the exciting news to Jesse, who brought in his six eldest sons for Samuel to choose from.

Samuel looked over the first, who was tall and well built, but decided he was not the one. The second was also a fine specimen, with all of the outward attributes which would make him a great king; but Samuel rejected him too, along with the four remaining eldest sons.

When Samuel then asked Jesse if he had more sons, Jesse apologetically told him he did have one more son, David, but that he was the family runt assigned to the task of tending sheep.

Samuel insisted on seeing David and immediately chose him as the future king, although Israel's current king was still reigning.

Put yourself in David's shoes for a moment. From all indications it appeared that David's family didn't think much of him, choosing to exclude him from the initial lineup. This family's attitude had more than likely wounded David's opinion of himself and left him wondering if he was good enough to do anything significant in life. But then, out of nowhere, Samuel appeared and revealed that God's purpose for him was to be king of the greatest nation on earth.

With this new sense of his destiny, David headed out to the battlefield where Israel was at a standoff with its archenemy, the Philistines, to take his brothers some food and check on their well being. When he arrived, he found all of Israel cowering in fear because the Philistines had a giant named Goliath fighting for them. And rather than have a bloody massacre resulting from both armies' fighting one another, the Philistines had proposed that Israel send its best man out to fight Goliath. The loser and his respective side would then be sentenced to servitude for life.

However, no one stepped forward with the courage to confront the giant Goliath.

But when David arrived with the care package for his brothers and heard both Goliath's taunts from the valley separating the two sides and news of the reward the king had offered to anyone who would go out and defeat the giant, he bravely volunteered.

When Eliab, David's oldest brother, heard David's bravado, he immediately challenged his motive: *"Why did you come down here? And with whom have you left those few sheep in the wilderness? I know your pride and the insolence of your heart, for you have come down to see the battle."And David said, "What have I done now? Is there not a cause?"*[31]

Notice the question Eliab asked David, which was essentially "What are you here for?"

This is what God is asking *you*: "What are you here for? What is your reason for existence? What have you been placed on earth to do? Are you here to take up space, or are you here for a specific purpose?"

If you're going to overcome grasshopper mentality, you will have to discover the answers to these questions.

Also notice the next thing Eliab said: "I know why you're here, David. You are here to watch."

In effect, David's response to this was "Listen, I'm not here to watch or to check things out. I came here to do what no one else wants to. I am here to do the work of kings, to protect and defend their kingdom and people! I came *to participate and to fulfill my purpose*."

What was true for David is true for you too. God didn't place you here on earth to be a spectator. Your purpose is not to be an observer, but a *participator* in the work of His Kingdom.

---------- ❖ ----------

You are not called just to watch, but to actively participate in God's overall plan for this world by fulfilling your purpose

Armed with the knowledge of why he was created, David

began both thinking and acting like a More Than Conqueror. When King Saul tried to discourage David from going out to fight Goliath by saying, "You are not able to go against this Philistine to fight with him; for you are a youth, and he a man of war from his youth,"[32] the More Than Conqueror in David responded, *"Your servant used to keep his father's sheep, and when a lion or a bear came and took a lamb out of the flock, I went out after it and struck it, and delivered the lamb from its mouth; and when it arose against me, I caught it by its beard, and struck and killed it. Your servant has killed both lion and bear; and this uncircumcised Philistine will be like one of them, seeing he has defied the armies of the living God."* Moreover, David added, *"The Lord, who delivered me from the paw of the lion and from the paw of the bear, he will deliver me from the hand of this Philistine."*[33]

Energized by his newfound purpose, David's More Than Conqueror mentality went with him onto the battlefield as he squared off against Goliath. Seeing David, who was just a teenage boy, Goliath laughed and jeered, *"Am I a dog that you come to me with sticks? Come to me and I will give your flesh to the birds of the air and beasts of the field!"*[34]

But unfazed, David continued to think and speak like the More Than Conqueror he was: *"You come to me with a sword, with a spear, and with a javelin. But I come to you in the name of the Lord of hosts, the God of the armies of Israel, whom you have defied. This day the Lord will deliver you into my hand, and I will strike you and take your head from you. And this day I will give the carcasses of the camp of the Philistines to the birds of the air and the wild beasts of the earth, that all the earth may know that there is a God in Israel. Then all this assembly shall know that the Lord does not save with sword and spear;*

for the battle is the Lord's, and he will give you into our hands. "[35]

So, empowered by his purpose and fueled by his More Than Conqueror mentality, David did the impossible, defeating Goliath and winning his place as Israel's next king!

THE PRIZE OF PURPOSE

Purpose will define your goals, create a life message, develop your endurance, reward order and obedience, require uncompromising focus, reject confusion and doublemindedness, increase your confidence, produce a standard of excellence in your life, and generate an inner joy that will touch the lives of everyone who comes in contact with you.[36]

And the focused pursuit of your purpose will keep you on track as a More Than Conqueror, reward you with a sense of fulfillment, and guarantee that you reach your Promised Land.

But how can each of us discover his or her purpose? This is the subject of the next chapter.

Chapter Four

Discovering Your Purpose

Success without purpose is only achievement without fulfillment. You can have everything this world offers; but if you're not walking in your purpose, there will be an empty hole in your heart. An event in the life of a young man named Dr. Clyde Wilson illustrates this point.

The thunderous applause of the assembled crowd filled the air after the mayor made his announcement: "Ladies and gentlemen, it gives me great pleasure to present the Outstanding Citizen of the Year award to Dr. Clyde Wilson, Jr. for his distinguished service to this community."

A well-built, clean-cut young man rose to his feet and walked confidently to the stage. Sitting at the table he had left were his father, Mr. Clyde Wilson Sr., and his mother, Emily. It was the moment they had waited for all their lives—to see their son become all that *they* had ever envisioned for him. As pride filled their hearts, they knew no one else in the room could possibly understand their sense of accomplishment, satisfaction, and fulfillment.

Mr. Wilson had always dreamed of being a medical doctor, and when Clyde Jr. was still quite young, his father had told him he would do whatever it took to see ensure his son could become the doctor, which he himself had never been able to be. Young Clyde's parents had labored at many jobs over the years and had lived without many of life's conveniences just to make it possible for their son to attend medical school and complete his internship. This evening made their sacrifices worthwhile, as Clyde junior now brought honor and respect to the family.

As Dr. Wilson stood on the stage, holding the plaque, the members of the audience rose to their feet, cameras flashed, and shouts of adulation filled the room. Then the applause subsided as everyone waited for the young doctor's comments. For a moment he stood erect, poised to speak. Suddenly his composure broke, and, with tears flooding his eyes, he pleaded with his parents in a loud voice that echoed the despair in his eyes, "Please, Mom and Dad, forgive me. I'm sorry, but I can't go on."

Bewildered and embarrassed, the chairman helped the doctor off the stage. The audience was shocked, wondering what could possibly have spoiled this triumphant moment for the successful young doctor.

As Clyde and his parents drove home, Clyde tried to explain the cause of his uncontrollable behavior to his perplexed parents, describing the frustration that had built up within him over the past ten years. "Everything I've accomplished has been done to please you, Dad, and to fulfill your lifelong dreams. I've become what you wanted me to be, but I have never become who I am," he said. "In spite of all the cars, homes, and other material things I now have, my life is empty. I never wanted to be a doctor as you did, Dad. I actually hate being a doctor. I always wanted to be a musician, but you and Mom wouldn't let me follow my dream."

Please understand. I love and respect you deeply. I'm aware of all the sacrifices you've made to give me my education, and

I thank you for it. But tonight I realized I just can't continue living to fulfill your dreams and expectations. I've got to start fulfilling my own. When I accepted the award tonight, I felt like a hypocrite. Someone I don't even know earned that award because I don't know myself. I want to live. I want to come alive. I want to be what I was born to be. Please set me free and let me live."[1]

This painful but necessary turning point allowed him to pursue his destiny.

If you will walk in your purpose, God will add the benefits. The book of Proverbs tells us, *"God's blessing makes one rich, and he adds no sorrow with it."*[2] There is none of the emptiness experienced by Dr. Clyde Wilson. We can look at our material possessions and tell ourselves they are nice and that we enjoy them, but they are all just "stuff."

---- ❖ ----

The reason many people become attached to material objects is because they obtained them outside of their purpose.

If they had been acquired in the quest of their destiny, it would be a different story. Why? Because the pursuit of their purpose would be what truly fulfilled them rather than the material possessions accumulated along the way.

But when people attain success without purpose, their earthly wealth is everything to them, and, as a result, they become tight-fisted. If God said to them, "I think I need to use your possessions for such and such a purpose," they would respond, "Oh, no, Lord! You don't know how hard I have worked! I labored in college and graduate school for eight years to get where I am today, and I was finally able to purchase this nice home and this new car. Lord, don't ask me to give them up for *anyone* or *anything!*"

Again, people fall in love with their "stuff" because they have never fallen in love with their *purpose*. God has equipped us to succeed in our calling. If we stray outside of it and make a decision to do something *we* prefer instead of what *God* has called us to do, we won't have the equipment we need to succeed. This means we can achieve true success only in the pursuit of the purpose for which God created us.

The Gospel of Luke challenges us to this end: "For what profit is it to a man if he gains the whole world and is himself destroyed or lost?"[3] *Himself* refers to the essence for living— the purpose for which a person was created. In other words, what does it benefit a man if he gains everything but never fulfills his purpose?"

Success [by God's standards] has very little to do with what you accumulate, possess or achieve. It has even less to do with other people's opinions and their assessments of you and your accomplishments. *Success can only be defined by purpose and measured by obedience.*"[4]

Purpose is the *reason* for the creation of *anything*, the "why" behind its existence. It is what *motivates* the manufacturer to create his product. Getting the item to do what it was intended to accomplish is the fulfillment of the reason for its existence. Similarly, following through on the purpose God had in mind when He created us is both an indication of obedience and a promise of success.[5]

God measures our achievement not by what *we* have done compared to what *others* have done, but by what we have done compared to what we were *supposed* to do. Success is really a matter of being who we were born to be. As Dr. Myles Munroe states, "You are not successful just because everyone says you are. You are not successful just because you have done what others have expected you to do. You are not successful just because you receive commendation and recognition from your peers or the accolades of the masses. You are truly successful only if you have done what you were put on this earth to do."[6]

—————— ❖ ——————

Purpose is the key to fulfillment in life; consequently, existence without it has no meaning.

Without purpose, we feel no passion for living and never have a reason to wake up in the morning. It gives us an inner assurance of importance and value—and is why it helps us overcome grasshopper mentality.

A <u>DISCOVERY</u>, NOT A <u>DECISION</u>

Our working definition of purpose is simply this: Your purpose is the unique mission which God intended for you as an individual when He created you. As we have seen, the Lord didn't just assign you a mission after He formed you. He had an ultimate destiny in mind *when* you were born, and He equipped you from the beginning with all of the qualities and abilities you need to fulfill the task. And pursuing and achieving your divinely intended assignment will guarantee that you won't see yourself as small and insignificant.

Learning how to discover your purpose, therefore, is a vitally important step towards achieving an overcomer's mentality. And *discover* is the right word for the endeavor—because you need to *discover*, not to *decide* what motivated God to create you—the purpose He had in mind. As God told Jeremiah, "Before you were in the womb, I knew you and called you to be a prophet unto the nations."[7]

103

When you were a child or a teenager, people probably asked, "What do you want to be when you grow up?" They were asking for an answer, however, they didn't understand that you would need to discover what *God* had created you to do.

Your answers to the following four questions can help you as you seek to find the Lord's purpose for your life:

1. What do you love to do?

What you really enjoy doing is evidence of a talent or predisposition God has instilled in you—a gift that may be dormant, but nevertheless suggests your uniqueness. What you love also reveals a curiosity and sensitivity others may not share.

When I was nineteen years old, that very question led me to the discovery of my purpose. Having been a youth leader for three years and sensing God's call into ministry full time, I was asked by my pastor to preach at the Sunday evening service. Although I was extremely nervous, I accepted and began preparing diligently. I studied all week and practiced more times than I can remember, even rehearsing my sermon over and over using furniture as an audience.

The day arrived, and it was time for me to preach my first sermon ever to adults. I remember it as if it were yesterday. My title for the message was "Grace and Gullibility— Perfect Together."

Fighting back my jitters, I walked up to the platform, stood behind the pulpit, and began. Then, after only two minutes into my forty-minute sermon, I felt an amazing grace wash over me that calmed my nerves and caused the words I was speaking to flow freely. The feeling of overwhelming joy was astounding. At that moment I came to know my purpose—to teach God's precious Word for the rest of my life.

Many overlook that first purpose-revealing question (What

do I love to do?) because they believe God will force them to perform what they really don't want to, or they have no interest in pursuing. But there is a difference between God requiring us to do something that we aren't equipped for and the Lord asking that we do something we won't like in order to chip away at our self-will. Since many people don't understand the difference, they do things they aren't interested in because they erroneously believe God has assigned those activities as their purpose.

———————— ❖ ————————

We feel empty when we're not doing what we have been called to accomplish and consequently what we will naturally enjoy doing.

And if we fail to discover our divinely intended purpose, we will fruitlessly seek to dispel the empty feeling either through material acquisition or by giving ourselves over to our materialistic desires.

A wonderful story by Isak Dinesen called "Babette's Feast" illustrates how doing what one loves overpowers all other pulls and passions. The story is set in a strict, dour, fundamentalist community in Denmark. Babette works as a cook for two elderly sisters who have no idea that she had once served as a chef to nobility in her native France.

Since Babette's dream is to return to her beloved home city of Paris, every year she buys a lottery ticket, hoping to win enough money to return. And every night her austere employers demand that she cook the same dreary meal—boiled fish and potatoes—because, they tell her, Jesus commanded, "Take no thought of food and drink."

One day the unbelievable happens: Babette wins the lottery! The prize is 10,000 francs, a small fortune. And because the anniversary of the founding of the community is approaching, Babette asks if she might prepare a French dinner with all the trimmings for the entire village.

At first the townspeople refuse: "No, it would be sin to indulge in such rich food."

But Babette begs them, and finally they relent. "As a favor to you," they tell her, "we will allow you to serve us this French dinner." But they secretly vow not to enjoy the feast, but instead to occupy their minds with spiritual things, believing that God will not blame them for eating the sinful meal so long as they do not enjoy it.

Babette begins her preparations. Caravans of exotic food arrive in the village, along with cages of quail and barrels of fine wine.

Finally the big day comes, and the village gathers. The first course is an exquisite turtle soup. The diners force it down without enjoyment. But although they usually eat in silence, conversation begins to take off. Next comes the wine—Veuve Cliquot 1860, the finest French champagne. And the atmosphere changes. Someone smiles. Someone else giggles. An arm comes up and drapes over a shoulder. Someone is heard to say, "After all, did not the Lord Jesus tell us to love one another?"

By the time the main quail entrée arrives, the austere, pleasure-fearing people are giggling and laughing and slurping and guffawing and praising God for their many years together. The pack of Pharisees is transformed into a loving community through the gift of a meal. One of the two sisters even goes into the kitchen to thank Babette, saying, "Oh, how we will miss you when you return to Paris!" But Babette replies, "I will not be returning to Paris, because I have no money. I spent it all on the feast."[8]

Babette's passion was to prepare the finest cuisine and see

people enjoy her creations. So, when given the opportunity to do what she loved, even her sudden windfall became a servant to her true love—cooking.

We too can find this same power in doing what we love, thereby allowing God to bring His blessings into our life for us to richly enjoy.[9]

———————— ❖ ————————

God wants us to do what we love.

As one of the Psalms admonishes us, *"Delight yourself also in the Lord, and he shall give you the desires of your heart."*[10] If we remain yielding and compliant in God's hands, He will plant His desires in our hearts. In other words, we will find ourselves loving to do what God calls us to do! Passage after passage in the Bible assures us that God wants our joy to be complete.[11] So why would He ask us to do anything we find unpleasant or hateful?

Children, still unspoiled by society, seem to understand this naturally.

As a father and his small son were about to leave Disneyland, the little boy begged, "Can I have another ride on Space Mountain?" When the father refused, with the excuse that he was out of money and they were out of time, the little boy surprisingly came back with "Jesus wants me to go. When we were in church, you said that whatever we feel, Jesus feels. When we cry, He cries. You said Jesus feels every emotion we have. If He feels every emotion, then when I'm laughing on Space Mountain, He's having a good time too! I think He would enjoy it if I had another ride on Space Mountain."[12]

Not bad theology. We all need to learn to do what we really enjoy!

2. What makes you angry?

We have been told too often that emotions are unproductive feelings which are to be suppressed. But God intends us to feel with our senses *because they help us to accomplish our purpose.*

Emotions are always involved whenever our faith is at its strongest. When our heart is involved in activities dictated by our faith, we have a greater motivation to stand fast until we have achieved our goal.

---❖---

Our inner feelings are detrimental to us only when we allow them to block us from being guided by our faith.

But even emotions such as anger, that we have been warned against as negative, can have a positive purpose. What makes us upset can call our attention to what we have been called to correct. Anger can be important because it can inspire an inner passion for righting wrongs. For example, when Jesus saw the moneychangers plying their trade in the temple, it was His wrath which motivated Him to right the wrong, throwing over the tables of the moneychangers and declaring, "My house shall be a house of prayer!"[13] Like Jesus, when we harness our anger and use it productively, it can and often does propel us forward.

Many years ago during a Knicks-Bullets playoff basketball game, one of the Bullets came up from behind the great Walt Frazier and punched him in the face, whereupon the referee unfairly called a foul on Frazier. But instead of allowing his anger to overcome him, Frazier didn't complain. His expression never changed. He simply called for the ball and put in seven straight shots to win the game—an *amazing display of productive anger.*[14]

So don't ignore or push aside your outrage, because it just may be one of God's directional signs intended to help you discover your true purpose.

3. What makes you cry?

Two different people can witness the same distressing thing, but one person may walk by, seemingly unmoved, while the other stops and weeps with compassion.

What makes us cry reveals what we have been called to heal. Jesus openly wept with compassion when He heard that Lazarus was dead—and through this faith was born which motivated Him to call forth Lazarus from the tomb.[15]

As it was with Jesus, the issues that move *us* to tears can also prove to be pivotal for us in discovering our purpose. This was true for Lynette LeGette, who lived in Louisville, Kentucky, where 21,800 patients each year receive chemotherapy treatments, causing most of them to lose their hair.

Learning about this brought tears to Lynette's eyes. And when she also learned that patients would complain about being cold during the night and wrap pajamas or towels around their heads to keep warm, she devised a plan—one she at first thought might be too overwhelming a project for her to carry out.

Lynette's idea was to create turbans for cancer patients who had lost their hair. Some of her first creations went to a mother in Kansas, for whom she made a number of caps for both winter and spring. Later, when Lynette met the woman's seven-year-old daughter, the little girl wrapped her arms around Lynette's legs and told her, "You made my mom so happy! She has a hat to go with every outfit!"

Lynette has become known as the Hat Lady. Since the summer of 2002, she and her now six volunteers have made well over 1,000 turbans, providing them free of charge to those in need. Lynette is a modern day Dorcas. "When you ask the Lord what you should do," she says, "you need to be willing to listen for the direction and recognize the opportunities He gives you." In many instances these opportunities may be initiated by emotions which tug on your heartstrings.[16]

Don't ignore your tears or broken heart. You can turn your distress into action, allowing your compassion to propel you toward your purpose! Your faith can be translated into results when your emotions are engaged.

4. What have you been gifted to do?

This is the final and most crucial question you should ask yourself in your search to discover your purpose. What have you been gifted to do? What can you do well?

The natural talents we possess are an important guide in the quest for our purpose because success in the pursuit of any goal is always dependent on certain innate abilities. For instance, owls have the natural gift to see in the dark because God created them to gather their food at night and to sleep during the day. Spiders have the ability to spin webs because this is how they snare their food. Woodpeckers have strong beaks so they can chip away at tree bark in order to get to the insects they need for nourishment.[17]

And since God is a perfect Creator, He would naturally provide us with whatever means we need to accomplish our intended mission. You and I need to look within ourselves, therefore, in order to discover our purpose and be careful not to let ourselves be distracted by our envy of the special abilities of others, ones *we* obviously don't share. Your own special gifts are a determining guide to your intended purpose. So if you can't sing, you're not called to be a singer. If you can't teach, you're not called to be a teacher. Your *own* gifts constitute one of the most crucial clues in your search for your personal God-intended purpose. Scripture teaches this truth plainly: "Let's just go ahead and be what we were made to be, without enviously or pridefully comparing ourselves with each other or trying to be something we aren't."[18]

God has given each of us the talent to do certain things well. So if the Lord has given you the ability to prophesy, speak out when your faith tells you that God is speaking through you. If your gift is serving others, serve them well. If your gift is to encourage others, do so with a smile! If you have money, share it generously. If God has given you leadership qualities, take the responsibility seriously. And if you have a gift for showing kindness to others, do so gladly.[19]

KNOWING GOD

Although the answers to these four questions are paramount in the discovery of our purpose, knowing God is an even more necessary requirement for discovering our reason for being.

———————— ❖ ————————

To find your purpose, you need to get close to your Creator so He can clarify your thinking by sharing His thoughts with you and imparting His passion in you.

God wants us to know Him more intimately than just by what we hear in church on Sunday morning. He longs for us to communicate with Him more than just through the prayers we bring to Him in our hour of need. He wants us to speak to Him more personally than just the two or three sentences we say about Him when we're leaving church on Sunday and everyone is watching.

God yearns for us to commune with Him more closely than

by the grace we say at our dinner table because we want to set a good example for our children. God wants us to have a personal awareness of who He is. We must know Him intimately if we are ever going to discover our purpose. The reason is simple: Only God knows why He created us.

THE PURSUIT OF WISDOM —THE PRINCIPAL THING

The apostle Paul was able to both discover and to finish his course because of his closeness with God.[20] And just as it was true with Paul, when knowing the Lord becomes *your* passion, God will reveal the reason He created you. His wisdom will become *your* wisdom. And true wisdom derives from knowing what God knows and it leads to doing what He would do.

The book of Proverbs tells us of the most important thing we can seek: *"Wisdom is the principal thing; therefore, get wisdom. And in all your getting, get understanding. Exalt her, and she will promote you; She will bring you honor, when you embrace her. She will place on your head an ornament of grace. A crown of glory she will deliver to you."*[21]

Why is God's wisdom the principal thing? Why does it cause promotion in our lives? Why does it bring honor and favor? The reason is that it leads to the discovery of our purpose and the knowledge of how to accomplish it.

When God told Solomon, "I will give you anything you want —just ask Me," Solomon answered, "I want wisdom."[22] What he really meant was he desired to know what God knew concerning how to fulfill his purpose. Solomon was no fool. He knew that if he could understand how to fulfill his purpose, there would be no limit to the blessings he could experience.

THE PASSION TO KNOW GOD

The conclusion is a simple one. If your burning passion is to know God, you will discover your purpose. Of course, it is easy to *say* you want to know the Lord; but how can you be sure if you are truly *passionate* about knowing Him.

This question reminds me of a story concerning the response the ancient Greek philosopher Socrates gave to one of his students when the young man asked his mentor how one acquires knowledge. "Come with me, son," said Socrates, who then led the fellow down to the ocean shore, where they waded out to where the water was chest deep. Then, without warning, Socrates pushed his student's head under water and held it there long enough to cause alarm before releasing him and asking, "What do you want?"

"Knowledge," gasped the breathless young man.

Not satisfied with his answer, Socrates repeated the dunking several more times, each time holding the poor fellow's head under water a bit longer, following the dunking with the same question and eliciting the same answer—"I seek knowledge."

Finally, when the boy was half drowned, Socrates received the answer for which he was waiting. "What do you seek?" asked the mentor. "I want *air*!" gasped the student. "I want *air*!"

"*Now* you have it!" cajoled Socrates. "When you come to want *knowledge* as much as you now want *air*, you will have knowledge!"

All of us need to have a similarly breathless passion to know God, a subject we will take up again at the close of this book

So earnestly seek to commune with your heavenly Father, and you will discover the purpose He has envisioned for you that will bring out every strength, every gift, and every character trait He has uniquely bestowed upon you. No longer will you view yourself as a grasshopper. Armed with your newly found purpose, you will begin to see yourself as a More Than Conqueror, full of potential.

CHAPTER FIVE

KNOWING YOURSELF
AS PURPOSE-DIRECTED

We are all aware we have more potential than we actually take advantage of, but we need to learn how to make full use of it. In the book of Philippians we are told this from the apostle Paul: *"But one thing I do: Forgetting what is behind and straining toward what is ahead, I press on toward the goal to win the prize for which God has called me heavenward in Christ Jesus."*[1]

RELEASING YOUR POTENTIAL

Clearly God is telling us that our intended course is integrally connected to what we think, so *controlling* our thoughts is paramount. A race car driver revs his engine just before beginning a race to assure himself that his motor has the potential power to win for him. Similarly, seeing ourselves as God sees us—in the light of our purpose—is like that race car driver testing his engine, because we are reassuring ourselves we have power in reserve for dealing with every challenge we may encounter on life's dangerous road.

The book of James gives us the first key to releasing our unused potential by reminding us, "Faith without works is dead."[2] God is prompting us to understand that the first thing we have to do to in this process is *try*.

The book of Proverbs reminds us that *"a righteous man may fall seven times and rise again."*[3] This means that although we often fail on the first attempt, our failure can actually be a good thing because it helps us understand how to approach a task more intelligently, thereby bringing us closer to victory. So the second step towards releasing our potential is to *try again*.

Third, *we must refuse to quit,*[4] knowing that dogged determination is often all it takes for us to realize what we are capable of. This is illustrated in the life and legacy of one of the world's greatest novelists, Sir Walter Scott.

Scott, who once wrote, "I often wish that I could lie down and sleep without waking, but I will fight it out if I can," was a man who refused to give in. In his fifty-sixth year, failing in health and with his wife dying of an incurable disease, Scott was in debt for half a million dollars because a publishing firm in which he had invested collapsed. He might have declared bankruptcy but didn't because of the stain on his reputation this would bring. So he chose only to ask his creditors for more time.

So began his race with death; a valiant effort to pay off the debt before he died. To be able to write free from interruptions, he moved to a small rooming house in Edinburgh, leaving his dying wife Charlotte behind in the country. "It withered my heart," he wrote in his diary, but he knew that his presence could be of no further help to her.

A few weeks later, after she died, he wrote in his journal, "Were an enemy coming upon my house, would I not do my best to fight, although oppressed in spirits; and shall a similar despondency prevent me from mental exertion? It shall not, by heaven!"

With a tremendous exercise of will, he returned to the task, stifling his grief. Although stricken twice with paralysis, he labored steadily until his death in 1832, completing *Woodstock*,

Count Robert of Paris, *Castle Dangerous*, and other works. Having lost his mental powers at the time of his death, he mercifully died, happy in the illusion that he had repaid his debts —an illusion which miraculously turned to reality when, in 1847, they *were* finally paid with the sale of all of his copyrights.[5]

———————— ❖ ————————

If we give up along the way, we will never know what it is to enjoy the fullness of our potential in God.

As long as we refuse to abandon our purpose, we will eventually reap the blessings of our Promised Land.

Fourth, we are naturally motivated by rewards; so, while we also need to be aware of the possible *consequences* of our actions, we must consider and be inspired by the benefits we can expect if we release our full potential.

Look again at the story of David and Goliath. Most of us know that David defeated the giant with a few rocks and a slingshot. Few of us, however, realize what it was that motivated David. Many assume this driving force was a deeply spiritual one, such as his righteous indignation over Goliath's open mockery of God's people. But the Bible bluntly affirms that David was spurred on by the reward offered by King Saul, to anyone who would defeat the giant. Saul had promised great riches plus the hand of his daughter and a lifelong exemption from taxes to anyone who slew Goliath![6] When David heard of this, then and only then did he volunteer to take on the Philistine warrior.

Just as David fought Goliath because of his knowledge of the reward he would receive, we too need to be motivated by our knowledge of the abundance we will be given if we fully serve

God with all the potential He has placed within us.

Fifth, *expect to succeed.* Remember that before charging onto the battlefield to face Goliath, David went to a nearby brook and picked up five stones in anticipation of Goliath's four older brothers' becoming involved in the conflict. David had the mindset of a victor, believing that if a sibling cavalry tried to run to Goliath's defense, they too would fall by the stone! And like David, all of us must move forward expecting to win.

Sixth, *we need to surround ourselves with people who consistently remind us that we have potential and can succeed.* Problems or obstacles can sometimes make us feel as if we're up to bat in a tied ball game, with the outcome entirely dependent on our success or failure. In times like this we need fans in the grandstands who stand up and shout encouragement, confident we can turn the tide. Their support boosts our own self-confidence and determination, increases our adrenaline flow, sharpens our focus, and reinforces the power of our swing— just enough to let us belt a winning home run!

❖

Just as a baseball team's players need enthusiastic fans who believe in and encourage them, we must all surround ourselves with More Than Conqueror friends who support and consistently encourage us to make use of our potential and believe in us as winners.

The movie *Cinderella Man* tells the true story of boxing legend James J. Braddock (Russell Crowe), who made an incredible comeback during the Great Depression, inspired in part by the encouragement of his wife. Injured and arthritic, Braddock was facing the likelihood of having his career cut short, and he had to go on public assistance when he couldn't find work at the docks in New Jersey. But when an opportunity came for him to get back into the ring and provide for his family, he took it. And his world changed.

Once again fighting with a purpose, Braddock started winning fight after fight. He inspired the struggling nation with his perseverance in the midst of hardship. And as his comeback gained momentum, he kept remembering the faces of his children and his wife and how essential it was for him to provide for them. He finally won an opportunity for a showdown fight with the World Heavyweight Champion, Max Baer.

Baer, a vicious fighter who was notorious because two of his opponents died as the result of his powerful punches, ridiculed, threatened, and mocked Braddock in the days before the fight; and as the world looked on, concern for Braddock's life mounted.

When the big day arrived and just moments before the fight, Braddock's wife surreptitiously sought out her husband in the arena's locker room. The look on her face sent everyone else from the room as she went straight up to Braddock and, with a tender fierceness that could come only from a loyal wife, commanded her husband's attention for the last words he would hear before the big event.

"So you just remember who you are," she admonished. "You're the Bulldog of Bergen and the Pride of New Jersey. You are everybody's hope, and the kids' hero. And you are the champion of my heart, James J. Braddock."

Braddock won the fight.[7]

All of us need people in our lives who embolden us to make use of our full potential.

WHAT SIGNIFICANCE DO WE HAVE ON EARTH?

Let me emphasize again, the most crucial factor in releasing

God's vision for us is that *we must know our purpose.* The deepest craving of the human spirit is to understand why we are here on earth—our purpose and its relevance. We want to feel our lives count for something and that we matter. It is a need common to all of us, whether we are male or female, rich or poor, educated or not, black or white, young or old.

------------ ❖ ------------

Worldly success and wealth are not necessarily indications of who we are, why we are here, what we were born to do, what our potential is, or where we fit.

We can possess all the material trappings of success and still be victims of grasshopper mentality because significance and relevance are directly dependent on *purpose*, and without it we are ensnared in mediocrity.

Rather than an *acquired* attribute, purpose is *inherent*. Just as the manufacturer of a worldly product designs it to fill and successfully carry out a specific purpose, God instills a unique purpose within each of us before we are born, along with all of the qualities, abilities, and characteristics we will need to *fulfill* His plan.

A critical turning point occurs when we experience the motivation and power which comes with discovering our God-ordained objective and begin to focus on pursuing it until it is a reality.

PURPOSE GIVES LIFE MEANING

Without knowing the Lord's divine design, our lives are little more than meaningless blurs of activity—like stationary rocking horses, generating a lot of motion but never really going anywhere. As Solomon, the wisest man who ever lived, comments after observing how men live their lives chasing only after their personal needs and interests, a life that isn't directed by purpose is "Meaningless! Meaningless!"[8] Without a true mission, life is no more than a passionless existence.

Sir Winston Churchill, Britain's great World War II Prime Minister, whose indomitable will and bulldog determination both sustained his country's collective morale and played a key role in the ultimate triumph of the Allied Nations over Hitler's tyranny, had an life-altering experience earlier in his youth that powerfully illustrates this point.

Churchill saved a frail old man from drowning. Once the young swimmer had managed to get both of them safely onto a beach, the man he rescued shouted at him, "Why did you save me? Why didn't you let me die?"

Young Winston, who had known the man for years and admired him as a role model, knowing that he had amassed a vast fortune and had risen to the top in the business world, was perplexed. "But sir," he stammered, "why would you possibly want to die?" The old man's answer was a pivotal factor in changing the younger man's outlook on life.

With tears in his eyes, the old man buried his face in his hands and lamented, "What was it all for? What have I gained? I have everything and yet nothing. Everyone thinks I'm a success, but I'm not. I have made my parents happy and proud of me, and my wife has everything she could desire. My children want for nothing, and my reputation among my friends, associates, and enemies is impressive. Still I'm empty, depressed, frustrated and sad. My life is meaningless.

"Everyone knows *what* I am, but I don't know *why* I am. I've always been so driven by a desire to acquire things in order to impress others with who I am that I've never given any real thought to who I want to be for *myself*, to my personal *purpose* in life, or to how my existence could affect others. So today I decided that I'd rather die than continue to go on so pointlessly."[9]

The disillusioned old man was a tragic example of what can happen to a life sidetracked by grasshopper mentality. Finally overcome by an awareness of the purposelessness of his life, he saw self-destruction as the only path left open to him.

———— ❖ ————

When we are not fulfilling our purpose, everything dies within us and our lives become hollow and without significance.

Grasshopper mentality leaves us with little more than recurring doubts about who we are, whether our lives have any true meaning, and if anyone would miss us if we suddenly disappeared. But purpose has the opposite effect, making us resilient in spite of any and all obstacles.

This is the effect that knowledge of an ultimate plan had on Thomas Edison, who *knew* he had been born to be an inventor. His creative genius devised the microphone, the phonograph, the incandescent lightbulb, the storage battery, talking movies, and more than 1000 other marvels.

In December of 1914, at the age of sixty-seven, he had been working for ten years on a storage battery—a project that had greatly strained his finances. One fateful evening spontaneous combustion broke out in the film room, and within minutes all the packing compounds, celluloid for records and film, and other flammable goods were in flames. Fire companies from eight surrounding towns arrived, but the heat was so intense and the water pressure so low that the attempt to put out the fire proved futile. Everything was destroyed. Within minutes all of Edison's assets went up in flames. And although the damage was in excess of two million dollars, the buildings had been insured for only $238,000 because they were made of concrete and had been considered fireproof.

The inventor's twenty-four-year-old son, Charles, frantically searched for his father, finally finding him calmly watching the fire, his face glowing in the reflection, his white hair blowing in the wind.

"My heart ached for him," Charles later commented. "He was sixty seven—no longer a young man, and everything was going up in flames. When he saw me, he shouted, 'Charles, where's your mother?' When I told him I didn't know, he said, 'Find her. Bring her here. She will never see anything like this again as long as she lives.'"

But when Edison looked at the ruins the next morning, his reaction was characteristically upbeat: "There is great value in disaster. All our mistakes are burned up. Thank God we can start anew." And three weeks after the fire, Edison managed to deliver the first phonograph.[10] His secret for maintaining such resilience was that he knew his purpose!

"Purpose is the master of motivation and the mother of commitment. It is the source of enthusiasm and the womb of perseverance. Purpose gives birth to hope and instills the passion to act."[11] It is the key to fulfillment and consequently to gaining the assurance that our lives are meaningful and of value. And the task of fulfilling our God-given vision is uniquely our own.

PURPOSE BRINGS NEW UNDERSTANDING

Once we know the Lord has a design for our life, we come to understand two vital truths which help us overcome grasshopper mentality and release our God-given potential. The first is that we are important because the Almighty created us, so our very existence is sufficient proof that the world needs something we potentially have to offer. God is a God of purpose, and everything He creates is brought into existence for a reason.

The second thing we come to understand is that we are fearfully and wonderfully made, with qualities and talents which are uniquely our own. Provided with this awareness, we can rid ourselves of the grasshopper mindset that has held us back and live our lives fully and meaningfully, rejoicing in the knowledge we are on the ordained path that will take us toward the personal goal God has set for our future.

DON'T BASE YOUR LIFE ON COMPARISONS

People who base their lives equating or comparing themselves to others develop the ten scouts' kind of grasshopper mentality. They tend to think of the abilities and qualities of others as more significant and consequently superior to those God has given to *them*. For instance, you might look at a successful person and think he or she is smarter than you, or had better educational opportunities. But you need to remember that God has also equipped *you* to be successful as you pursue the fulfillment of your special mission. The Lord needs you because you are an essential part of His plan just the way you are. No one else has your personality or your particular combination of gifts and talents.

So we need to celebrate our uniqueness. Booker T. Washington once commented that "[whatever we fail to celebrate] becomes common, comfortable, and easily taken for granted, or yet, even worse, completely overlooked." He also observed that "[excellence] is to do a common thing in an uncommon way."[12]

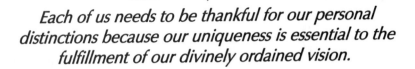

*Each of us needs to be thankful for our personal
distinctions because our uniqueness is essential to the
fulfillment of our divinely ordained vision.*

No one else can accomplish the mission God has assigned specifically to *us*.

This truth reminds me of the parable-like story of a race involving a rabbit, a squirrel, and a duck which included stages that required running, swimming, and climbing. The rabbit was obviously good at running, the squirrel at climbing, and the duck at swimming. But each member of the team was applauded for his individual gift. Even though the rabbit couldn't climb, the squirrel couldn't swim, and the duck couldn't run, each knew enough to excel at what he *could* do. As a result, each achieved his own measure of success, allowing his differences to *define* him instead of *confine* him.[13]

Our individuality is a tool God has given to equip us for success. No wonder David was able to say with such conviction, *"I will praise you, for I am fearfully and wonderfully made; marvelous are your works, and that my soul knows very well."*[14]

So be happy and rejoice in the fact God has created you to be an "original," because your uniqueness is what makes you who you are!

JESUS—MASTER OF THE UNCOMMON

The Lord was perfectly successful at fulfilling the reason for which He was born—and the Master of the uncommon. During His ministry on earth Jesus also taught and empowered others to attain success by taking advantage of uncommonness. In his book *Discovering the Power of Purpose*, Dr. Paul Crites cites twelve different ways in which Jesus was exceptional in attitude and action.

1. Jesus gave people uncommon directions.

Consider the guidance Jesus gave to two tired fishermen who had fished all night and caught nothing. He said to them, *"Launch out in the deep and let down your nets for a catch."*[15] It stands to reason that an extraordinary God would give uncommon directions that we cannot fulfill without relying on His supernatural power. The truth is, if what we have received from the Lord seems unclear, we probably haven't yet found our purpose.

2. Jesus asked uncommon questions.

To the man who had been ill for thirty-nine years, Jesus asked, "Do you want to be made well?"[16] This is an unusual question suggesting Jesus' ability and His willingness to carry through only after receiving a positive response!

3. Jesus noted uncommon contributions.

He watched as many people cast their large offerings into the temple treasury. But concerning the poor widow who came to the temple and put in two mites, Jesus said, *"Assuredly, I say to you that this poor widow has put in more than all those who have given to the treasury."*[17]

4. Jesus noticed and gave credit to uncommon faith.

When the Roman centurion told the Lord, "I'm not worthy for You to come under my roof. Only say the word, and my servant shall be healed," Jesus answered, *"Assuredly, I say to you, I have not found such great faith, not even in Israel!"*[18]

5. Jesus called people in uncommon ways.

He interrupted the two brothers named Simon and Andrew as they were fishing and called out, *"Follow me, and I will make you fishers of men."*[19]

6. Jesus was uncommon in His unbiased acceptance of others.

When the tax collector Zacchaeus climbed up in a tree to get a better glimpse of the Master, He turned to him and said, "Zacchaeus, I'm coming to your house today."[20]

7. Jesus both possessed and recognized an uncommon touch.

When the woman who had suffered from an issue of blood for twelve years touched the hem of His garment, He turned around and said, *"Daughter, your faith has made you well. Go in peace, and be healed of your affliction."*[21]

8. Jesus gave uncommon commands.

He arrived four days after the funeral of his friend Lazarus. But instead of grieving with the rest of the mourners, He stood before Lazarus' tomb and spoke with authority, "Come forth!"[22] *That* was an uncommon command.

9. Jesus made uncommon requests.

A crowd of five thousand men, plus women and children, followed Him to a mountainside to hear His teaching. Afterward, the disciples wondered, "How are we going to feed them all?" Jesus answered by making an uncommon request: *"YOU give them something to eat."*[23]

10. Jesus gave uncommon credit.

The disciples criticized the woman who broke her alabaster

box and anointed Jesus' feet with expensive ointment: "What a waste! We could have sold that ointment and given the money to the poor!" But the Lord answered, "Let her alone. Don't trouble her. She has done a good work for me."[24]

11. Jesus gave uncommon promises.

The resurrected Christ told His disciples, *"Behold, I send the promise of my Father upon you; but tarry in the city of Jerusalem until you are endued with power from on high."*[25] This one uncommon promise opened a door to the supernatural in a way that had never before been available to God's people.

12. Jesus had uncommon responses.

When the crowd of religious leaders wanted to stone the woman caught in adultery, Jesus effectively put a stop to the violence with His quiet response: "He who is without sin should cast the first stone."[26]

Again and again, God's Son used the uncommon to advantage and He empowered others by causing them to recognize their own unique gifts. In the same way, the Lord wants us to be aware that *we* too have an uncommon purpose to fulfill. When we discover this, we will no longer make the mistake of judging ourselves negatively because of our differences. Instead, we will begin to celebrate our distinguishing characteristics as essential to the fulfillment of the ultimate plan God intends for us.

CONFIDENCE BORN OF PURPOSE

Another advantage of knowing our mission is that an awareness of it gives us confidence. We develop a More Than Conqueror attitude which assures us that we have the potential needed to overcome everything.

———— ❖ ————

When we know why we were placed on this earth, we also grow confident in the knowledge that following the heavenly plan ensures divine protection.

Psalm 91 describes this promise from God:

He who dwells in the secret place of the Most High shall abide under the shadow of the Almighty.... Because you have made the Lord, who is my refuge, even the Most High, your dwelling place, No evil shall befall you, nor shall any plague come near your dwelling. For he shall give his angels charge over you, to keep you in all thy ways.... With long life will I satisfy him and show him my salvation.[27]

If our heavenly Father has promised His people longevity and supernatural protection, why do so many fail to walk in this security or live extended lives? One primary reason is that they are not following their purpose.

When we are intentionally following God's divine plan for us, no weapon formed against us can prosper—*not one.*"[28] It is pointless even to try to discourage someone who knows his purpose and is following it because he is dwelling "in the secret place of the Most High" and "under the shadow of the Almighty."

In the Gospel of Luke we find an example how God keeps His children safe. Jesus and His disciples were on their way to the other side of a lake when out of nowhere a storm arose that threatened both to destroy the ship they were on and their lives. Although the disciples were professional boatmen, they were nevertheless very frightened and began to panic. But when they looked around to see where Jesus was, they found Him in the lower part of the boat, asleep on a pillow! They awakened Him and asked for His help, whereupon Jesus calmly rebuked the life-threatening tempest, causing a great peace to come over the waters.[29]

Why was Jesus able to remain so peaceful when confronted by the storm while His disciples were gripped by fear?

——————— ❖ ———————

Jesus lived free from anxiety not because
He knew He was divine, but because He knew
He was following a divinely ordained plan.

He fully understood He was not destined to die in the storm. His purpose was to die on the Cross to redeem mankind from sin and to reconcile us all to the Father. Jesus had an assurance the storm couldn't harm Him because His destiny lay elsewhere. As a result, faith sustained Him, allowing Him to speak with authority and subdue the stormy sea.

The same confidence and feeling of security will prevail in *your* life as you walk in your purpose. You will journey through life with the commanding power of faith, free from all fear because you know you are destined to fulfill what God has ordained for you.

ESCAPE THE TRAP OF YOUR COMFORT ZONE

Many people never experience the peaceful rest and realization of their potential because they continually exist outside of their purpose. If this continues for a protracted period of time, we usually need to find someone or something which breaks us free—otherwise, where we are becomes a comfort zone because of its familiarity. If this happens, breaking loose is difficult, even if we're unhappy, dissatisfied, or unfulfilled, because we are frightened by the thought of what we may find on the other side.

A comfort zone can be a very dangerous place in which to be trapped. Think back to the Israelites' dilemma. Although the people had been slaves in Egypt, when things became uncomfortable in the wilderness, their former land was perceived as a safe place where they longed to return. They cried to Moses, "Why did you take us out of Egypt? We want to go back there. At least we were fed!"

Well yes, the children of Israel had food in Egypt, but Pharaoh provided only enough to make them feel comfortable and not rebel. God had to send a deliverer to shake them up and set them on the road to freedom—even if leaving their familiar surroundings meant accepting some discomfort along their way to fulfilling the destiny God had planned for them.

The longer you ignore the Lord when He urges you to abandon your pleasant lifestyle and pursue the purpose He has ordained, the harder it becomes to obey and the greater price you may have to pay for your hesitation. What we sow we will reap is a universal law, and so is the opposite: If we fail to sow, there will never be a harvest.

If we tarry too long in our familiar surroundings, we may acquire enough of what we erroneously think of as benefits and blessings to make us even *more* reluctant to break free, knowing we may have to put up with being *less* comfortable at least for a while) if we make a change. And if we continue to delay and become even more complacent, God may shake us up by taking away some of the deceptive "blessings" and benefits we think we have.

As some of the pseudo advantages are stripped away, we may conclude God is being unjust and unfair. But in such a situation, the Lord is only nudging us to pursue the purpose that will lead us to our intended destinies.

Before God's intervention, we allowed our lives to be defined by something entirely irrelevant to God's vision for our future. As the Bible tells us, the Lord God is at work in us to will and to do according to His good pleasure.[30] And His good pleasure is to lead us to fulfill His intent for our lives.

─────── ❖ ───────

God had to get Moses' attention in order to push him onto the path towards purpose fulfillment.

When Moses learned that someone had seen him kill the Egyptian, he thought, *I need to get out of here! They're going to catch me, and bad things are going to happen!* So he left the ease and prestige he had enjoyed in Egypt and fled to a mountainside, where he met his future wife and began to tend his father-in-law's sheep.

There, as a shepherd, he had time to ponder how far he had fallen from his previous position of honor. He probably thought, *I used to live in Pharaoh's palace. I was living in the lap of luxury. But here I am, tending sheep on the back of a hill!*

It was only after Moses was stripped of all signs of worldly success that he encountered God, who appeared to him in a burning bush and defined his purpose: "I want you to go back to Egypt, but this time I want you to go to Pharaoh's house and deliver my children from bondage."[31]

Like Moses before God appeared to him, you may be going through an uncomfortable time right now as God endeavors to prod you into your purpose. If this is true, remember that the journey toward your ultimate destiny probably won't take off speedily the second you embark upon it. If you are wandering in the wilderness of life, walking outside of God's design, remember that the Lord is just as committed to you as He was toward Moses, and this may mean He will have to jolt you out of your comfort zone.

We occasionally have to endure a little shaking in order to make us recognize our potential. It's how eagles learn to fly. When a baby eaglet is born, the mother picks out a safe spot to build her baby a nest, way up on the mountain cliffs. At first she lines it with her soft down-like feathers to protect the eaglet from the pricks of the sharp branches that make up the nest. Then, each day, she brings the baby three of the best square meals she can find.

But as the eaglet begins to grow, the mother starts stirring up the nest. She pulls away all the soft feathers to cause her baby to be pricked by the branches and be motivated to attempt to fly. Then, seemingly cruelly, she jumps into the nest, violently flapping her wings and pushing the eaglet out of the nest and over the cliff. And in response to its sudden distress, the baby eaglet begins to flap its own wings, discovering it can fly— and ultimately to soar.

Like the mother eagle, God sometimes stirs up our comfortable "nests" in life so that we can realize our potential and reach our Promised Land!

CHAPTER SIX

LIVING YOUR PURPOSE

Your life probably won't change overnight when you discover why God created you because your purpose still has to unfold over a period of time. But you can hasten the task of bringing it to light by doing your part in order to win the battle of the mind. To rid yourself of grasshopper mentality so you can experience the fullness of your reason for being, you have to renew your mind and think differently.

For example, grasshoppers look at current situations and ask "Why?" More Than Conquerors dream things that never were and ask "Why not?" Grasshoppers tell themselves, "I'm not going out on that limb; it's too risky."More Than Conquerors confidently reassure themselves, "Why not go out on the limb? That's where the fruit is!" Because these two groups of people think uniquely, they experience completely different levels of achievement, success, and fulfillment.

To reach our individual Promised Lands, we must first achieve a state of mind and positive perspective on life that will allow us to be everything God has created us to be. Great battles must be won in the mind before they can be won in life, and to have victory in conflict, we must entertain the right mentality.

BREAKING FREE OF THE DEVIL'S SHACKLES
The apostle Paul alludes to winning the battle of the mind in

Second Corinthians when he instructs us to cast down imaginings.[1]

The word *imagining* suggests a blockage where we remain in bondage as a result of poor thinking—a vain figment of the imagination that is not true but is empowered by the thoughts with which we feed it.

But if we think correctly, we won't be bound in any area and will be able to resist these vain imaginings before they become pitfalls.

Some people are skeptical about the possibility of living a struggle-free existence. They look at themselves and say, "Well, I have ninety-eight percent of everything working well, so that's a pretty good percentage. I doubt that I can do any better."

But you can!

———————— ❖ ————————

You can lead a life liberated from every form of bondage, but accomplishing this will depend on your thinking.

If you've ever seen a circus performance, you've probably marveled how trainers can make elephants do almost anything they want them to. Elephants weigh several thousand pounds each, but two relatively puny humans are able to control their movements completely during a performance!

The reason is revealing. When a future circus elephant is very young and not yet strong, its trainer ties one end of a rope around one of its legs and the other end around a tree. At first the baby elephant will strain and struggle against that rope. But because its strength hasn't yet developed, it can't break free. After awhile, the young elephant learns that trying to break the rope is futile; so it stops struggling.

Later, when the animal is fully grown, the trainer is able to tie a rope around one of its legs and attach the rope to a small stake. Despite the fact that the now-powerful elephant could almost effortlessly break the rope and walk away, it remains tied to the stake, convinced that breaking free is impossible.

Psychiatrists call this type of conditioning "learned helplessness"—the acquired pattern of negative thinking which can prevent not just elephants, but any of us from even trying to liberate ourselves from the mental trap that holds us hostage.

In a study carried out by psychologists at the University of Chicago some years ago, two groups of people were isolated in separate rooms. Those in one room were exposed to the noise of loud, recurring gunshots fired every fifteen seconds over a thirty-minute period. The people in the other room were exposed to precisely the same sort of noise torture, but with the angry, irritating sound of barking dogs instead of gunshots. The subjects in both of the rooms were hooked up to electronic equipment that enabled the psychologists to monitor the responses of their nervous systems during the thirty-minute exposure.

Next, the two groups were again separated and isolated for another experiment, but this time in noise-*free* rooms, where they were instructed just to *imagine* the same persistent noise (of either the gunshots or the barking dogs) for another thirty-minute period, with the psychologists once again monitoring the responses of their nervous systems.

The data from the experiment revealed that the agitated nervous responses to the remembered or *imagined* noises were identical to those registered during the *actual* noise exposure.[2]

The outcome of the experiment illustrates another kind of learned helplessness. We can become conditioned in such a way that we can experience and react mentally and emotionally to *imagined* stimuli, even when there is no *external* cause. For instance, we may not have succumbed to a former bad habit for a number of years; but because we long ago conditioned ourselves to give in when the urge arose, we remain in danger of a relapse. Our learned helplessness will continue to keep us in bondage until we discover how to cast down vain imaginings and change our way of thinking.

Many of God's children act like that full-grown elephant tied to a small stake by a slender rope. The enemy's traps have no real power over them, but they stay in subjection because of their own state of mind. Believers need to realize that the devil's "ropes" don't have any real dominion over them anymore! God wants you to be free, not to think like a grasshopper.

YOU HAVE A COURSE, NOT A CAREER, TO FULFILL

Discovering our purpose is only our *initial* mission. Our *ultimate* goal is to follow our assignment according to God's plan and thereby bring our purpose to fulfillment. We can do any number of *right* things during our time on earth, but unless we fulfill what God intended and created us to do, we will *not* hear "Well done, good and faithful servant"[3] when we stand in judgment one day.

The apostle Paul *knew* he would hear those words when *he* stood face-to-face before Jesus and the Master asked him to account for his days on earth. Reflect once again on what Paul said as he neared the end of his earthly life: *"I have fought a good fight, I have finished my COURSE."*[4]

You may think you are pursuing a career in your chosen field, whether it is business, medicine, law, or whatever. But if *all* you have is a career, you haven't yet found your God-intended course. Your training may have equipped you to get started toward your objective, but it is *not* your course. So if *all* you are doing is pursuing a career, life hasn't even *begun* to take on true meaning for you. You need to pursue what God created you to do!

ACTIVE PURSUIT OF YOUR PURPOSE KEEPS HOPE ALIVE

Discovering God's ultimate vision is an essential first step, but actively *pursuing* it in order to realize its benefits is an equally essential *next* step. If all you do is find your purpose without ever *experiencing* it, grasshopper mentality will return.

---❖---

The enemy will begin to play mind games with you again because he understands your thought life is the battlefield where your victory or defeat will be determined.

The devil will whisper, *Did you actually think you are good enough to make what you've been dreaming come true? It was just a self-made fantasy! It had nothing to do with why God created you. After all, look at the baggage you're carrying around from the past. Look at your shortcomings. God would never choose a person like you to do what you've been dreaming! Also, if that dream is really your purpose, why hasn't it come true yet?*

The Bible says it this way: *"Hope deferred makes the heart sick, but when the desire comes, it is a tree of life."*[5] As time passes and you haven't experienced the fulfillment of the desires God has placed in your heart, deferred hope will eventually challenge your faith and your overcomer's mindset. This is why you must start taking deliberate steps in the quest of your purpose. You won't reach your destiny overnight, but active and dedicated pursuit of your God-given vision will keep hope alive in your heart.

Remember, as time ticks away and we fail to reach our targets, we can easily fall back into a grasshopper mentality which is unable to recognize blessings when they come our way.

The story of golf legend and instructor Harvey Pennick accurately illustrates this point.

Pennick bought a red spiral notebook in the 1920s and began jotting down observations about golf. He didn't show his book to anyone except his son until 1991, when he shared it with a local writer and asked if he thought it was worth publishing. The man read the book and left word with Pennick's wife that he did indeed think it should be submitted to a publisher.

In the days that followed, Simon and Schuster agreed to publish Pennick's book with an advance payment of $90,000. But the next time the writer whose advice Pennick had sought saw Pennick, the old man seemed troubled, explaining to the writer that with all of his medical bills, there was no way that he could advance Simon and Shuster the money the publisher had requested.

The writer had to explain to Pennick that *he,* the *author,* would be the one to receive the $90,000. His first book, known as *Harvey Pennick's Little Red Book: Lessons and Teachings from a Lifetime in Golf,* sold more than a million copies. It continues to be one of the best-selling books in sports-writing history. His second volume, *And If You Play Golf, You're My Friend,* sold 750,000 copies.[6]

We must not stop at discovering the path God has planned, we have to start moving toward the goal. Otherwise we could duplicate Harvey Pennick's first reaction as an author; a blessing can come our way, and we won't be ready to receive it, thinking we are not deserving.

SOW THE SEEDS FOR YOUR HARVEST

Living out your purpose will provide you with a perpetual

140

harvest, but only if you are faithful in sowing seeds. The concept involving the relationship between sowing and reaping is one of those universal laws God desires us to be aware of and to make use of in our lives.

He reminds us of this law in Genesis and Galatians: *"While the earth remains, seedtime and harvest, cold and heat, winter and summer, and day and night shall not cease"*[7] and *"Do not be deceived; God is not mocked: for whatever a man sows, that he will also reap."*[8]

Harvests result only from seeds that are sown.

--------------- ❖ ---------------

What happens to us today is the outcome of what we sowed yesterday—and what we experience tomorrow will be a result of what we sow today.

But whatever seeds you plant in life, make sure to assign purposes to them. Think of your seeds as *anything in your present situation you can assign to work for you in your future.* Plant you seed in fertile ground so they can grow and work for you. As Ecclesiastes reminds us, if we cast our bread upon the water, it will soon come back to us on every wave![9]

FIVE WAYS TO SOW OUR SEEDS

The first seed we can sow toward the fulfillment of our purpose is one of good old-fashioned hard work. As a verse from Proverbs tells us, *"He who works his land will have abundant food, but the one who chases fantasies will have his fill of poverty."*[10]

❖

*If you fail to work your land, you will never
experience your intended harvest.*

Some people just sit around dreaming of the future, waiting for the Lord to give them their golden moment. They pray, "God, I know You put that dream in my heart ten years ago. So why haven't You brought it to pass? Make it happen, Lord!" They seem to assume they should be able to achieve fulfillment without becoming personally involved in working or contributing to make their dreams come true.

But the Bible tells us very directly that a person who doesn't labor on his land will not enjoy a harvest. Your purpose is your "land" —your reason for being on earth. If you work it, you will experience abundance.

Working to fulfill your purpose with dedication is a requirement for reaching your destiny. Patience plus the sweat of your brow is necessary before you can materialize your dream.

Don't become a "couch potato," excusing your inactivity by deceiving yourself that your future is entirely at the mercy of either fate or God. The truth is, laziness is the primary reason so many people fail to reach their objectives and reap the rewards the Lord intends for them. Sluggish individuals miss out on the prize because they waste time twiddling their thumbs or choosing to do only what they feel like.

Following our dream always requires effort. In his book *Fuzzy Memories*, Jack Handey addresses the issue: "There used to be this bully who would demand my lunch money every day. Since I was smaller, I would give it to him. Then I decided to fight back. I started taking karate lessons. But then the karate lesson guy said I had to start paying him five dollars a lesson. So

I just went back to paying the bully. Too many people feel it is easier just to pay the bully than it is to learn how to defeat him."[11]

The same is true when it comes to fulfilling our calling. Many would rather give in to the temptation to sit idly by than to sow the seed of hard work and reap its blessings. Do not depend on God to shower you with riches and grant fulfillment without your involvement.

FAITHFULNESS

The second seed we can all sow to experience our purpose is the seed of faithfulness. We can't constantly roam from one project to the next and be successful. In order to produce and achieve as God intends, we must put down roots. Just as trees can't grow and bear fruit without having a healthy root system, neither can we.

At least four things happen when we continually disrupt our lives and leave one place for another. First, we disturb the soil and interrupt the rhythm of the lives of our family members and of everyone else around us.

Second, every time we uproot, we leave behind a vacuum, an empty space. It takes time both to repair the damage and to transplant ourselves somewhere else in order to once again be fruitful.

Third, we diminish our resources. When we uproot, we usually have to deplete our assets to effect the change, often holding up our pursuit of purpose while we strive to recover our losses.

Fourth, we halt all production of fruit—and must replant and restart the growing process.[12]

Turkeys, believe it or not, can teach us a lesson regarding sowing the seed of faithfulness. Male turkeys, often referred to as toms or gobblers, are created with a unique ability. When a tom gobbles, all hens within range answer the call and move toward him. During the spring mating season, toms signal for potential mates all day long.

There is an exception, however. If a tom already has a hen with him, most of the time he will not leave his lady to seek out another, no matter how enticing the temptation might be. The tom is "programmed" to know that females come to him. In most instances, a mature turkey will not leave the hen he can see to chase down one he can't. Doing such is against his nature. However, there are exceptions.

From time to time a tom will violate his programmed instinct to be true to his mate and leave her in quest of another. If this happens, the wayward tom will usually have sealed his fate—because what sounded to him like a willing partner was probably an imposter holding a gun. A tom that stays with his lady is virtually guaranteed to live out his days in contentment.[13]

—————— ❖ ——————

Faithfulness is often the vital seed which makes it possible for us to accomplish what God created us to do.

Of course, there are times the Lord moves us from one arena of life to another—from one occupation to another, or one church to another and we must obey.

So the admonition concerning the pitfalls of uprooting is directed solely to people who constantly move by whim or just because something occurs they don't like. Maybe they didn't get their way on an issue. Perhaps they didn't agree with an action their boss or pastor took. They allow whatever causes their displeasure to uproot them.

Such individuals never know the joy of living out their purpose.

EXPERIENCE THE REWARDS OF MENTORSHIP

A third place where we need to plant a seed is in a godly mentor. Each of us can benefit greatly by the guidance of such a person because there is great power in the miracle of mentorship. Biblical history illustrates this when we examine the relationship between Joshua and Moses. Consider these questions:

- Why was Joshua the one whom God chose to lead the children of Israel into the Promised Land?
- Why was Joshua able to do what Moses could not?
- Why was Joshua the one whose faith parted the Jordan River?
- Why was Joshua able to lead the Israelites in defeating the giants?
- Why was Joshua the person who lived to enjoy the land which flowed with milk and honey?
- What was it about Joshua that enabled him to experience such a magnificent purpose?

Simply put, Joshua first served as Moses' *minister*.[14] Although the word minister can mean either *assistant* or *slave*, the intended meaning in this instance is *assistant*, but with the implication that a clear student-mentor relationship existed between Joshua and Moses—one that both inspired and taught Joshua, thereby enabling him to rise to the heights and lead God's people in victory into the Promised Land.

In order to come into the fullness of your purpose, you must learn to welcome and profit from the power and influence of a mentor in every aspect of your life.

Example after example in the Bible tells of these

145

relationships and the great impact a mentor had on his or her student's life. Throughout Scripture, those who learned and grew under such tutelage were the ones who were able to perform unparalleled exploits for God.

Elisha was responsible for many more miracles than Elijah. Mentored by Naomi, Ruth became part of the lineage of Christ. Because of Paul's mentorship, Timothy came to lead the Church of Ephesus, the largest church in biblical times. And with the guidance of Moses, Joshua was able to lead the children of Israel into the Promised Land. Seeking and accepting mentorship is a necessary seed we can sow to help us reach our destiny.

A mentor must, of course, be spiritually mature; but he (or she) must also be mentally and emotionally sound enough not to be intimidated in any way as he helps you to develop your natural gifts.

Anyone you can intimidate cannot be
your mentor because your undeveloped abilities
will never be able to blossom under the guidance
of his obvious grasshopper mentality.

Your chosen counsel must also be someone whose counsel is backed by personal experience, because this is the most vital attribute of a true mentor. This fact is what Paul (the mentor) had in mind in his counsel for Timothy (the student): *"And the things that you have heard from me among many witnesses, commit these to faithful men who will be able to teach others also."*[15]

A mentor can be defined by three primary characteristics:

First, the individual must be able to provide you with an exit from your present and an entrance into your future. He or she must be someone who "has been there and done that" and is consequently familiar with roads and avenues of which you aren't yet aware—and of the detours and distractions along the way.

Second, a mentor must have the confidence and sense of accomplishment *you* too must cultivate. Attitudes, whether good or bad, are *contagious*; so you need to associate only with those who possess a positive outlook and who will encourage both trust and achievement.[16]

Since both bad and good perspectives tend to rub off on others, if you are a parent and consequently a mentor for your children, you should continually convey self confidence and an optimistic outlook to them. Never let them hear you complain, for instance, you are experiencing financial hardship. The family's finances isn't a childhood responsibility. "God will provide" is the attitude you should project. And when good fortune occurs or returns, you should always remind your children how the Lord has provided!

Third, your mentor must himself (or herself) possess the body of knowledge you will need. The familiar adage that "experience is the best teacher" is misleading. It is our access to divine knowledge which determines our progress and growth.

Of the two ways to learn in life, through *mistakes* or through *mentors*, learning through mentors is definitely the better choice![17] You don't always need to make errors in order to learn. Instead, take your mentor's advice when he says, "If you do that, it will be a mistake." It's not necessary to try to reinvent the wheel when we are considering a particular course of action. Instead, we should go to those who prayerfully mentor us with wise counsel. We need to tell them, "Here's what I'm thinking of doing. So I just need to ask you how *you* would handle this and whether my idea is the right course to take."

Then, if your mentor responds, "No, don't do that. I've tried it, and it doesn't work," then *you* shouldn't attempt the project. Of course, you also need to funnel the advice you receive through the wisdom and direction of God. But sowing the seed of mentorship will help you to avoid many unnecessary pitfalls.

CHARACTER IS EVERYTHING

Character—a small thing that makes a huge difference—is a fourth seed we must sow. Personality is the image we project to others—what we appear to be on the surface, and reputation is the collective opinion others have of us, for whatever reason. But our character is who we truly are.

A good and honorable character is an attribute we want everyone with whom we come in contact to have, but for which we personally aren't always willing to pay the price. Unfortunately, we are often more concerned by the lack of integrity and noble qualities in others than we are about our *own* deficiencies.

───────── ❖ ─────────

Character is the will to do what is right, as God defines it, regardless of the cost.

Proper concern for this is often a problem because we live in a society that seems to value achievement over character and where right is defined by advancement and wrong by whatever impedes it. Consequently, when faced with defining moments in our lives, we frequently choose achievement over character, ignoring the fact that in God's book the qualities of our inner man is an essential seed for us to plant in order to reap our destiny.

148

You may have heard of current Hall of Fame Washington Redskin's football coach Joe Gibbs and wondered about the secret of his success. He is also a race car owner and perhaps this story about his team's 2001 NASCAR Busch Circuit win at Talladega can shed some light on it.

The story involves a revelation that came to Crew Chief Tim Shutt, a relatively new believer who had encountered Christ at a Christian retreat for participants in the racing industry. It happened just in time to save him from being found guilty of cheating by making an illegal adjustment on the No. 20 car to be driven by Mike McLaughlin.

"Joe Gibbs [the team owner] was adamant that we not cheat," Shutt remembers. "But most teams figure that so long as you get away with it, it's not considered cheating. So I told Mike that morning in practice, 'If we're no good in practice, I'll put this piece—the illegal piece—on. Probably thirty other teams are doing it.' I was justifying my actions.

"I got under the car, I got halfway through putting it on, and that verse 'Seek ye first the kingdom of God' came flashing in red in front of me. And whoa, that was it. I said, 'I'm leaving this up to you, God.'"

Shutt didn't put the illegal piece on the car. And McLaughlin won the Talladega race, one of the biggest of the year.

"When we won, the first thing that came to my mind was that verse," Tim says. "God wanted to show Himself to me."[18]

As seen in the life of Joe Gibbs, our character has much to do with whether or not we reach the objective God has planned. As Emerson once observed, "Sow a character and reap a destiny." All of the greats seem to grasp this concept. We too must grab hold of this truth if we want to fulfill our mission and achieve greatness.

SOW SEEDS IN ANOTHER'S DESTINY

The fifth and final seed we can sow in pursuit of our purpose is the seed of assistance. The book of Ephesians tells us that if we do something good for someone else, God will repay us in like manner.[19]

A story about a poor Scottish farmer named Alexander Fleming illustrates this principle.

Fleming was working in the fields one day when he heard a cry for help coming from a nearby bog. He dropped his tools and ran toward the voice. There, waist-deep in the black muck, was a terrified boy, screaming and struggling, trying to save himself from sinking.

The farmer rescued the boy, pulling him from what would have been a terrifying death.

The next day a fancy carriage pulled up to the Fleming's house, and an elegantly dressed nobleman introduced himself as the father of the boy whom the farmer had dragged from the bog. The nobleman said, "I want to repay you for saving my son's life."

The farmer replied, "I don't want payment."

But at that very moment the farmer's son came to the door of the modest home, and seeing him, the nobleman said, "Let me repay you this way: Allow me to provide your son with the same education that my son will have."

The farmer happily acquiesced, "Yes, I will accept."

As a result, the farmer's son attended the finest schools in England, graduating from St. Mary's Hospital, the medical school in London, and going on to become famous around the world as Alexander Fleming, the discoverer of penicillin.

Years later, the nobleman's son who was rescued from the bog was stricken with pneumonia, and his life was saved by penicillin. The name of the nobleman was Lord Randolph

Churchill, and his son's name was Winston Churchill.[20]

This story demonstrates the power that sowing the seed of assistance can have on our destiny. So constantly look for those you can help, and do it with all your heart.

———————— ❖ ————————

Putting the law of sowing and reaping into motion for your future is not an option.

Your destiny is dependent on what you plant—and remember, if you sow no seeds, you reap no harvest.

DON'T DESPISE SMALL BEGINNINGS

Never forget, God wants the desires He has instilled in you to come to fruition. It is He who has given you the urge to achieve greatness.[21] The Lord wants you not just to *know* your purpose, but to *experience* it as well. The way you do this is by sowing seeds for your harvest—seeds of work, faithfulness, mentorship, character, and of assistance. So begin moving immediately toward the vision God intends for you, and as you do, God's mighty blessings will flow into your life.

However, on the road to your victory, don't despise the day of small beginnings. At first you may experience only a measure of what your heart tells you to do. If so, don't become discouraged. If you remain faithful to what God has called you to, He will take the small beginnings and transform them into greatness.

We often have to give God's purpose for us a chance to grow in order to be able to experience its fullness. So even though you may not be where you want to be today, keep pressing on. Just keep sowing the right seeds, and let the Lord do the rest. If you sow, someone else will come along and water the seed; and in the end, your storehouse will be filled and overflowing

In summary, we can see how God has fashioned our lives in three stages—the *discovery* stage where we come to know the nature of our destiny, the *sowing* stage where we sow the seeds for our destined harvest, and the *experience* stage where we walk in our purpose and fulfill our mission.

Even when we are on the road to our destiny, we must continue to sow seeds to guide us and illuminate the path that remains. As we are told in Proverbs, *"But the path of the just is like the shining sun, that shines ever brighter unto the perfect day."*[22]

If in any phase of your progress towards your objective, you feel less eager than you once were, remember that you are called to move from glory to glory, with your path burning brighter and brighter until you reach your intended goal! Also bear in mind you are ahead of where you used to be and that you must never look back. Move forward toward greater and greater achievement, never allowing yourself to become trapped in a comfort zone that keeps you from moving steadily in pursuit of your God-intended destiny. If you persevere in following the light the Lord shines on your path, the momentum of His power will become a mighty moving force nothing can stop!

CHAPTER SEVEN

LIVING A MAXIMIZED LIFE

J ust how far and how high can your potential in God take you? And what would your life be like if you learned how to live in "the maximization zone"?

To answer these questions, you must first understand this key point: *You have the potential to operate just like God.* As the Bible tells us in Genesis, He created you in His image and in His likeness![1] Just as God is a Spirit, so you are a spirit being. You don't only *have* a spirit—you *are* a spirit.

EQUIPPED TO FUNCTION LIKE GOD

Once you learn to see yourself as a spirit being, you will begin to understand your ability's potential. Think of it! God made you not only to *be* like Him; He made you to *function* like Him! This is what it means to be made in His likeness.

Of course, if you don't believe God created you; if instead you choose to believe you share your origin with monkeys and apes, then your potential will be limited in the same way as that of animals. But if you understand you were created in the Father's image, *God* becomes the measure of your potential. He is the mark toward which you aim.

Since God created you to function like Him, if you aren't,

you are *mal*functioning!

And the Almighty operates by means of *faith*. The Bible tells us that pleasing God is impossible without faith.[2] God never functions in fear. He never becomes frightened, worried or wrings His hands. He never asks Himself, "Is the purpose that I want to achieve really going to happen?"

———— ❖ ————

God doesn't become confused about
His will, and He is never influenced by dread.
He always functions through faith.

Fear is essentially the direct opposite of faith. This is why the Bible assures us, *"God has not given us a spirit of fear, but of power and of love and of a sound mind."*[3] Your thinking is solid only when you are functioning by means of faith.

But in addition to *creating* you to operate like Him, He also *equipped* you to do so. We are advised in Romans to think of ourselves "according to the measure of faith that God has given to each of us."[4] And faith is the equipment you need to operate as He does. It is His ability instilled within you—your internal assurance of greatness.

When you begin to think of yourself as a spirit being, fully capable of performing as God performs, you won't be able to hold on to grasshopper mentality even if you are tempted to do so!

EQUIPPED TO DOMINATE IN YOUR LIFE

One of the ways that you are equipped to function like God is found in the first chapter of Genesis where we are told the Creator gave us "dominion."[5] Like God, you have the potential to dominate, rule, and subdue. Outside of the Almighty, there is *nothing* that should control *you*. For example, God didn't create you to be influenced or addicted to cigarettes or alcohol. He didn't create you to be controlled by drugs, sex, money, power, or greed. He created you to control and overcome through His power and ability operating *within* you!

So the next time you're tempted, revolutionize your thinking. Begin to see yourself as someone who was created to be in control. Consider the danger and tell yourself, "You can't dominate me! I have power over you. There's no way this temptation is going to overwhelm this much heavenly power!"

EQUIPPED TO IMAGINE, TO PLAN, AND TO PRODUCE

We also have the God-like ability to imagine and plan anything we set our hearts to accomplish. This potential is also revealed to us in Genesis when the Lord said, "These people are working together because they all speak the same language. This is just the beginning. Soon they will be able to do anything they want."[6]

Of course, this was before God confused the languages of the people who were building the Tower of Babel. But on the Day of Pentecost, God restored to us the power of a unified tongue when He gave us a *new* language from heaven.[7] Now that we can speak heaven's vocabulary, we can once more imagine and plan to carry through on anything God summons our hearts to achieve!

EQUIPPED TO EXPERIENCE THE IMPOSSIBLE

Like God, we also have the potential to experience the impossible through the power of belief. As Jesus said, *"If you can believe, all things are possible to him who believes."*[8]

A woman by the name of Diane Dew tells of a time when her

five-year-old boy taught her this truth.

"As a single mother," she reports, "I often could not afford anything beyond rent and utilities. I had only $5, and we needed to buy milk and bread.

"When I told Jonathan, 'New tricycles are expensive, so let's pray and ask God,' in his childlike faith, he agreed.

"'What color trike do you want?' I asked him, explaining that God likes us to be specific when we pray so we'll know the answer is from Him.

"'Green, my favorite color,' he answered matter-of factly.

"'And we don't want a rusty one,' I added.

"I admit that I became a bit nervous about being so specific because my little boy's faith might be shattered if God didn't come through; but when I came to realize the source of my concern, I was able to put my fear aside.

"Always scraping to make ends meet, as a single mom I often took advantage of opportunities to teach my child how, even without money, we could be rich in faith, rich in good deeds, and rich in mercy. Many times, however, I probably managed to learn more from the experience than he did!

"We got into our old Chrysler and, since we had only $5, decided to visit a yard sale or two. 'Let's ask that it be at one of the first ones we go to so we don't waste a lot of time,' I said.

"At the first place we stopped, Jon began running up the driveway, yelling 'Look, Mom, my trike! My trike!' And before I could say anything, he had hopped on the green tricycle and was riding it in circles. It was in such good condition, I really didn't think it was for sale.

"'Some kid who lives here probably just left it in the yard,' I said, doubting. 'There's no tag on it.'

"'But it's green, Mom, and it's not rusty! It must be mine!' Jon argued.

"He was right; it wasn't rusty at all. In fact, it was in such good condition, I told him, that even if it were part of the yard sale (and not some kid's who lived there), it would certainly cost more than we could afford.

"'But Mom, we prayed!'

"Ouch! I felt that. I asked if the tricycle was for sale and, if so, how much it was.

"'Oh, that's been in the attic for years,' she said. 'We don't need it. How much were you thinking?'

"'Three-fifty?' I asked, almost apologetically, thinking about the milk and bread we would also need to buy.

"That was a ridiculous price, to be sure. I felt embarrassed to have even suggested it. We both glanced at Jonathan zooming around and around in circles on her driveway.

"'Sure, why not?' she agreed.

"And that's how Jonathan got his nice green trike.

"While I have never studied the basics of mathematical probability, I know the 'chance' of finding a green tricycle, without rust, under $5, at the first yard sale we visited, on that particular day, was quite slim.

"But 'nothing is impossible with God.'"[9]

DISCOVER YOUR POTENTIAL

To learn the extent to which we have been equipped to function like God, we must readjust our minds to our potential by opening our Bibles and finding out what God's Word tells us. So the next time you think that *you can't*, that *you will never be*, or that *you'll climb only so high*, open your Bible and find out what *God* says about you. When you do this, grasshopper mentality and all that accompanies it will fade away and become only a distant memory!

Negative thinking imposes on us a fallen countenance and a

diminished sense of confidence. But when we look into the Word, which can be described as "the perfect law of liberty," and find out what *God* tells us about ourselves, the revelation of who we are inspires us, and our faces begin to glow as the joy of the Lord floods into us. It is impossible to feed on His Word and remain sad, angry or afraid.

Determine to learn what the Bible says about you personally. You will be amazed at how fearfully and wonderfully made you truly are!

POTENTIAL IS MAXIMIZED THROUGH PURPOSE

As we have emphasized, everyone ever born on earth is here for a purpose. No one arrives by accident. Not one individual has suddenly appeared and caused God to say, "Oops! We shouldn't have let that one through!" There is a reason for your life. You were created to do something specific and special for God. And once you discover what the special "something" is, you will be able to realize your full potential, because *when purpose is discovered, it can be maximized.*

---❖---

If you fail to find your reason for being you will never be able to recognize some of the latent gifts, talents, and abilities hidden within you.

But when you ask God to reveal His vision for you, these gifts and the Lord's timing come into alignment and create a magical revelation—the moment when you truly understand that you're on earth to carry out a divine assignment.

You are here for only a relatively short period. And "time" is just a temporary interruption in eternity—which was before, and will always be. The instant you were conceived, eternity was interrupted, but it will resume once more after you are gone. So you are obligated to pass from this life having fulfilled your purpose on earth.[10] Then you will be able to stand in judgment one day and hear those words: *"Well done, thou good and faithful servant."*

Remember, God isn't concerned with how beautiful or handsome you look, how well you speak, or how many people like you. He isn't interested in the square footage of your home, the kind of car you drive, the amount in you bank balance, or the number of your investments. *God's concern is that you fulfill your purpose and in so doing discover that you have been called to be extraordinary—another key to living a maximized life.*

CALLED TO BE EXTRAORDINARY

If we are encumbered by grasshopper mentality, we can't grasp the truth that we are called to be special in God's sight. Instead, we are inclined to think of ourselves as unworthy to be recipients of God's blessings. But the Lord doesn't want us to live trapped in mediocrity because it is what we think we deserve or, worse yet, because it is the standard others have imposed on us.

It's been said, "Mediocrity is the spirit of average, the anthem of the norm, and the heartbeat of the ordinary."[11] As children of Almighty God, we are neither unimportant nor ordinary, and we must consequently strive to live in the full potential of all God created us to be!

Life *is* easier, of course, when we think all we're entitled to is mediocrity. When we succeed in breaking out of the mold and pursue something higher in life, others might be inclined to regard our passion for greatness as suspect or pretentious. But if they do, it is only because they simply don't understand we have finally come to know what God desires for us! If you haven't yet observed that kind of reaction from other people, you probably haven't striven to go beyond the normal and pursue greatness. You've accepted the status quo—just having and being and doing what everybody else has, is, and does.

But when you *do* notice such a reaction, you should accept it as positive evidence of your progress! Remember, your value is not based on someone else's opinion of you. They can't define your aspirations. Your value and dreams come from understanding the assessment of your Creator—what He thinks about you.

---— ❖ ——

If you let other people's opinions dictate your life, you will remain trapped in below average living.

The Bible addresses the dangers of listening to man instead of to God: *"The fear of man brings a snare, but whoever trusts in the Lord shall be safe."*[12] The fear of man will prove to be *a snare* or *a trap of restriction.* But when we trust in the appraisal of our Creator, we will remain secure and on the right path!

Don't let yourself be a grasshopper, stuck in the rut of restriction and being average. "Within that devilish trap, you will be bound on the north by compromise, on the south by indecision, on the east by past thinking, and on the west by lack of vision."[13] But God doesn't want you to live there because *you are not ordinary.*

Lamentably, the world generally wants us to live "normal" lives, engage in "normal" activities, and associate with other "normal" people. They want us to have "normal" motivations and "normal" goals, to receive "normal" educations, and to live in "normal" houses.[14]

But living like this would be *tragic* because *you are not normal* or just ordinary. You are *extraordinary*. Therefore, you ought to:

- Lead an extraordinary life
- Engage in extraordinary activities
- Associate with extraordinary people
- Have extraordinary goals
- Live at an extraordinary pace
- Have extraordinary motivation
- Receive an extraordinary education
- Live in an extraordinary home
- Have extraordinary children
- And leave an extraordinary legacy

Nothing you do should be just ordinary! We need to remind ourselves at every point in life that we're not going to let *anyone* rob us of what the Lord has told us is ours. No one but God has the right to define us!

Grasshopper mentality is so pervasive in the world that a person has to do just a little bit extra in order to qualify as a "genius"![15] In fact, success in society seems to mean little more than hanging on after others have let go. All we have to do to be a top achiever is outlast the mediocre people who tend to give up as soon as things get rough.

God wants us to live a *maximized* life, escaping from the common trap called "average" and moving on to the uncommon level of "extraordinary"!

WE ARE CALLED TO DIE EMPTY

Another way to describe a maximized life is *to die empty*.[16] People would love to take their talents and gifts with them, but we have to leave everything behind when we depart this body. We won't need any trappings of our earthly life when we get to heaven, for there we will be perfect in every way.

You may notice how television sportscasters sometimes describe certain athletes as *warriors*. What they are suggesting is that these athletes expend all their energy, drive, desire, and ability during the game. They don't hold back any reserve for the after-game activities; they leave everything they have on the court or the field.

The earth on which we live is like an athletic arena. God has placed us here, and He wants us to make full use of all the skills, abilities and gifts within us in our fight to win the game! He wants us to *die empty*!

Note what the apostle Paul said at the end of his life: *"For I am already being poured out as a drink offering, and the time of my departure is at hand. I have fought the good fight, I have finished the race, I have kept the faith."*[17]

Paul likened his life to the priest's ceremonial drink offering in the temple service under the Old Covenant. Throughout the service at different intervals, the priest would take the ceremonial cup and pour out a little of its contents until the cup was completely empty.

Paul is giving us a very vivid image, suggesting that our lives represent cups of nourishment poured out on the world by our Creator. Your special vessel contains all of the wonderful, priceless treasures, gifts, and talents God has instilled within you. Every year, month, week, day, or hour holds an opportunity provided by the Lord for the pouring out of another portion of yourself until, with your ordained goal reached, you are completely empty.[18]

The Bible tells us that Jesus Himself died this way, having poured out His life unto death for the sin of mankind.[19]

Jesus gave everything He had. And if you want to make full use of what God has given you in order to fulfill *your* earthly mission, you will have to eschew the temptation to be part of the crowd and commit yourself to living a maximized life and to leaving this world empty.

Some people won't die this way *because they are resting on their laurels.* They live on what they did ten years ago, one year ago, or even yesterday. Very few are committed to doing something for God *today*, so they continue to bask in the glory of *previous* accomplishments.

———— ❖ ————

You must never allow what you've already completed to become more important to you than what you can still attain!

Sadly, some convince themselves that since they have already turned in what they consider to be their best performance and have achieved all that they *can,* they no longer need to press towards reaching the next goal God has set for them.

Pablo Casals, one of the world's greatest cellists, began his journey towards achievement when he was twelve years old. From that time on, he practiced on his cello every day for five hours without fail. By the age of eighty-five, he had accomplished everything anyone ever thought there was to achieve in his field. He had received numerous accolades and had become recognized as one of the world's greatest performers on his instrument.

One day someone asked him, "Pablo, why do you still practice five hours every day?"

"So that I can get better," was his simple reply.[20]

Casals achieved greatness because he understood a truth we also need to accept: We will never reach our full potential in this life. As long as we are here, we can always improve so that we can leave more of ourselves behind to bless others and further God's Kingdom on earth.

Another manifestation of limited thinking that will prevent people from dying empty occurs *when they become prematurely satisfied with current successes.* The world is filled with individuals who have overtaken some and surpassed the expectations of a few others—but who become satisfied with what they have achieved. From that point on, their standard of excellence is stuck in the status quo.[21]

Again, these are the *grasshoppers.* They may be doing better than most, but God wants them to excel! When you come to understand what the Lord knows you to be capable of and expects you to accomplish, you will know you can *never* achieve "enough"!

Just imagine what would have happened if Jesus had said, "Well, today I raised someone from the dead, so that's enough. I think I've reached the pinnacle of My ministry." Or what if He had commented, "I turned water into wine! No one can top that, so why shouldn't I just relax now and enjoy the reputation I've earned?"

Thankfully, Jesus didn't do this, but *some* people do! They think they have "arrived" when they reach a certain status in life, and their wrong thinking stops them from reaching their true destiny.

Yet another limited way of thinking occurs when people accept their current state as *the best they will be able to achieve under the circumstances.* This kind of grasshopper mentality assures them that considering everything they've gone through and all they are currently experiencing, they're doing the best they can.

People who think this way fail to see current events and conditions as no more than passing circumstances which are subject to change. Instead, they allow these situations to immobilize their God-given ambition and cause them to surrender to the present state of affairs.

COMFORT VERSUS PASSION

When our desire for comfort exceeds our passion for achievement, trapping us in our comfort zones, we also run the risk of not dying empty.

My life is currently successful and happy enough to trigger complacency. My ministry is going well, my church is in the top percentages nationally in both size and income level, and I have a marvelous marriage and wonderful children. I could let myself be content with where I am right now. If I stopped pressing to go farther in my call to the ministry, I would be able to spend more time with my family. I could even recycle my sermons from five years ago to save time in pulpit preparation. My life would certainly be more comfortable. But God won't allow this — *because my passion is greater than my comfort.*

————— ❖ —————

If you consistently avoid discomfort, you will always be trapped where you are, never moving on.

As you may recall from the illustration concerning how a mother eagle teaches her eaglets to fly, at times discomfort is good for us.

In the same way, God will sometimes cause us to be restless because He wants us to move on to the next level and maximize our lives. At times we will feel the pinch or the prick of the "sticks," which often come in the form of challenging circumstances. On other occasions God will step into our comfort zones and begin to flap His wings, disturbing us to the point we will realize we too have wings and are capable of flying high above mediocre expectations and average accomplishments.

When you begin to sense evidence of "divine discomfort," you have a choice. You can waste time feeling sorry for yourself and complaining about how uncomfortable you are until you find yourself falling to the ground, or you can flap the wings with which God has provided you and take your life to a higher level!

Grasshoppers take the first route, choosing to stay close to the ground—because they aren't high-flyers. They have wings, but they prefer to hop. They will fly a short distance, but they don't rise too far off the ground before they become uncomfortable and drop back to earth to start hopping again.

I'm sure you can name adults who prefer the grasshopper flying technique. They don't understand God has given them the kind of wings which will enable them to soar over every mountain which obstructs them.

THREE PRINCIPLES FOR ESCAPING MEDIOCRITY

There are three principles we can follow to escape from the mediocre crowd in order to live maximized lives: The Principle of Capacity, The Principle of Comparison, and The Principle of Experience.

The first principle states that *the true capacity of a product is determined not by the user but by the manufacturer.*"[22]

A man who was visiting Europe for the first time tells how

his host asked him, "How would you like to travel without speed limitations?"

The gentleman looked over at his host with a gleam in his eye and said enthusiastically, "I'd love to!"

So the two men took the host's car, with the visitor driving, and got onto the German Autobahn freeway, on which there is no speed limit. As the man drove, he looked down at the speedometer and saw he was going eighty miles an hour—the normal speed at which he was used to driving. But everyone else was passing him!

His host looked over and asked, "What are you afraid of? We're standing still!"

The man took this as a challenge and pressed on the gas pedal. Suddenly he was cruising at 115 miles an hour and whipping by other cars. He was King of the Road, Master of the Highway! He could even hear himself saying on the inside as he passed the slower-moving vehicles, "Why don't you just pull over and park and let a REAL driver come on by?"

But although he felt like the King of the Road, he was actually traveling at only 63.8 percent of the maximum speed of his vehicle, which had been designed to travel at a top speed of 180 miles an hour! So the true potential of the car was not realized by the speed at which the man was driving, nor was its potential in any way affected by the man's opinion of the car's capacity. The true capabilities had been built into the car by the manufacturer and was present whether or not the man chose to exploit it.[23]

You and I are like that car.

———— ❖ ————

*God created us to go at maximum capacity
in order to fulfill our purpose.*

This is not limited to or reduced by the opinions of others, nor is it altered by our past or present experiences. It has been predefined and "built" into us by our Creator. The nearer we draw to God, the more of a bond we develop with Him. And the stronger our relationship becomes, the closer we get to maximum performance capability.

Many people aren't even running at 63.8 percent of their capacity. They are running at 5, 10, 15, or 20 percent because it is the low standard set by those who are influencing them. Measuring themselves by the level of others within their sphere of influence, these individuals are content once they reach the level at which their peers are trapped.

———— ❖ ————

You must never allow others to determine your capacity or you will always sell yourself short.

Only you and God know your true potential. Many are performing and achieving below what is possible and are consulting with other people rather than with God concerning what is possible. As we've seen, this is what happened with the Israelites. They consulted with others about their capacity for inheriting the Promised Land. Since God had already told them that they could possess the land, why did they need to ask for a second opinion?

God has built a potential into us that others don't know how to measure. This is why people sometimes say things like "Why dream so big?" "You're arrogant," or "You really can't do that!"

How foolish we are when we allow such people to distort our concept of ourselves!

This was the Israelites' problem, and they didn't learn their lesson even after listening to and being misled by the ten scouts about their ability to conquer and inhabit the Promised Land. Before the Israelites made their big mistake, the ten scouts had already committed the error of talking with the giants regarding the extent of *their* capacity. But we should never confer with our enemies for a faith report!

Of course, the ten scouts never approached the giants in Canaan to ask them, "What do you think we look like?"—even though this is the impression we might get as we read the account in Numbers 13. They *did*, however, allow themselves to be distracted by their circumstances in determining whether they could go in and inherit the Promised Land. And when the older generation of Israelites embraced the ten scouts' evil report, they all found themselves continuing to wander in the wilderness rather than enjoying the land of blessing and favor God had promised!

The Lord's assessment of you is all that really matters. Your potential comes from Him and is much greater than you have imagined it to be. If you are going to escape from the prison of average and begin to walk in a maximized life, you will have to understand the principle of capacity.

The second principle that will help you leave mediocrity behind forever so you can live a maximized life is *the principle of comparison,* which reminds us that the only kind of comparing we should ever engage in is *what we have done measured against what we are supposed to do.*

One of the tragic mistakes we make in life is to measure ourselves against the standards, work, or accomplishments of another. Doing so puts our true potential at the mercy of others, giving them the prerogative to determine and define our success.

This kind of comparison can result in giving us either grasshopper mentality or an inflated ego.

The man driving 115 miles an hour on the Autobahn could at first have deceived himself by measuring himself against the other drivers, thinking that he was successful because he was passing all the other cars. Then later he could have deceived himself into thinking he was a failure just because someone else passed *him*. But the only true test of his success was the capacity at which he was traveling compared to the capacity of the car.[24]

In the same way, you need to measure yourself not against what someone else has done, but against the mission God has given *you*. Keeping pace with what the Lord expects is all that counts. It really doesn't matter how much money you make or how many people think you're successful. What does matter is that *you are on course with your assignment*.

The Bible summarizes the principle of comparison: *"For we dare not class ourselves or compare ourselves with those who commend themselves. But they, measuring themselves by themselves, and comparing themselves among themselves, are not wise. We, however, will not boast beyond measure, but within the limits of the sphere which God appointed us—a sphere which especially includes you."*[25]

What has God asked you to do? What has He equipped you to accomplish? That is your measure of comparison. If you want to break free from the ordinary, you will have to act on this principle by refusing to gauge yourself by anything other than what God has given to you.

The third principle you need to follow to escape from mediocrity into a maximized life is *the principle of experience*. It is given not to determine the limits of our lives, but to create a better life for us.

Referring back to the Autobahn, the driver's comments after his high speed adventure were profound: "Suddenly I had responsibility for power without externally imposed limits, and that produced mixed emotions inside of me, including temporary confusion. All I had learned from my past concerning restrictions imposed by the law as I knew it and the fear of violating speed limits began to wrestle with my newly found freedom. In essence, *the possibility of using maximum power was challenged by my learned knowledge of limitation.* I was a victim of the conditioning of my past and handicapped by the fear of unlimited possibilities."

The man's words speak to the fact that our past serves to condition many of us to run our spiritual race at a jogging pace of about two to three miles an hour. In other words, we run within the norm of what we know. But this mediocre pace isn't the standard by which we are called to run our race. God wants us to forge ahead according to our full potential! The fact that the man had never driven a car 150 miles an hour didn't mean the vehicle couldn't *go* that fast. This tells us *experience does not define capacity.*[26]

———————— ❖ ————————

Life lessons are not given to tell us what our limits are; they are given so we can understand how to lead better lives.

God wants us to go beyond where we are right now. So don't let experience limit you! Let it *empower* you!

All three of these principles have everything to do with your purpose.

First, our potential is determined by our Manufacturer. This is the principle of *capacity*.

Second, we can't reach our potential unless we pursue the standard that God has set for us. This involves the principle of *comparison*.

Third, as we pursue our purpose, we need to draw on our past and present in order to build a better future for ourselves. This is the principle of *experience*.

Purpose, then, becomes the key to breaking out of "average" so that we can run in the realm of the magnificent!

So step away from the multitude who just maintain the status quo and join the few who are committed to attaining their full potential by maximizing their abilities. Don't allow yourself to travel through life without accomplishing what you were born to do!

CHAPTER EIGHT

MADE IN THE IMAGE OF GOD

Have you ever seen the movie "Honey, I Shrunk the Kids"? It's a rather silly story about a scientist who invented a shrinking machine and then accidentally shrank his own children. One scene shows the youngsters—now about the size of ants—outside on the grass when they suddenly hear a lawnmower coming toward them and don't know what to do. They scream in panic and run for their lives. Because of their tiny size they're at the mercy of the oncoming lawnmower.

When you and I suffer from grasshopper mentality, we too can find ourselves acting like those ant-sized children, reduced to "small" people at the mercy of life's lawnmowers and therefore incapable of being everything God desires for us to be.

By now you probably realize that if you're going to be all the Lord envisions, you must forsake viewing yourself as a grasshopper and see yourself instead as God sees you—a crucial step toward achieving everything He has planned. And as we've learned, rather than judging us by our past, present, or future actions and accomplishments, God sees us as "More than Conquerors."[1]

We've also discovered that the evolution from grasshopper thinking to a More Than Conqueror mentality requires both hard work and dedication. As is true with any transformation, the first step is the most painful: we must be willing to look in the mirror and ask ourselves if our lives reveal grasshopper symptoms and, if so, take the necessary steps to rid ourselves of them.

- If our tendency is always to think of what could go wrong, we need to begin to look on the brighter side.
- If our tendency is to gravitate toward people who are always negative, we need to begin picking *new* friends who are generally positive.
- If our tendency is to obsess over what we don't have, we must begin instead to focus on being grateful for what we *do* have.
- If our tendency is always to look back, we must begin to focus on the good which lies ahead.
- If our inclination is to duplicate only what others do or have done, we must begin to focus on the unique dreams that God has for us as individuals.

Recognizing negative tendencies and taking steps to change is not always easy, but with God's help we can.

Once we've diagnosed grasshopper mentality and have decided to set ourselves on the path to thinking like a More Than Conqueror, the next step is mastering our environment. We do this by implementing the climate control principles we learned in Chapter Two. As you may recall, these principles are *taking control of our thoughts, overcoming our past,* and *putting our present in perspective.* Armed with these tools, we are well on our way toward obliterating negative thinking.

With our environment under control, we can focus on beginning to think like the More Than Conquerors which God has created us to be. As we read in Chapter Three, this involves *expecting victory and success in our lives, refusing to use excuses to explain failure,* and *embracing our God intended purpose.* These three steps will allow us to stay on course and ensure that grasshopper mentality remains conquered.

Accepting our God-intended purpose then becomes the key to unlocking the future the Lord has planned. Purpose, as we have seen, is the key to releasing our potential, giving meaning to our lives, and seeing ourselves as valuable and important— valuable because God thought enough of us to create us as part of His master plan and important because He has chosen us to fulfill a unique part of this plan. When we begin to see ourselves as purpose directed individuals, we become inspired to think big rather than small.

Even though at first we may believe that discovering our purpose is difficult, as we now know, it's really as simple as asking ourselves four life questions: What do we love to do? What makes us angry? What makes us cry? And what have we been gifted to do? The answers point each of us in the direction of our purpose—the very reason God chose to place us on planet earth.

———————— ❖ ————————

With our purpose before us and grasshopper mentality behind us, we can concentrate on experiencing the joys of living in our destiny.

What use is it to know why you've been created if you never *become* what God intended for you to be? To experience life in its fullness, you and I must follow the five steps we examined in bringing our purpose to light: work toward your purpose, lay down some roots and be planted, experience the miracle of a mentor, strive for excellence in character, and help others to accomplish their purposes. Taking these five steps will ensure that before long you will be living the victorious life the Father has planned. And when this happens, as we saw in the last chapter, you will say goodbye to mediocrity and hello to *superiority*!

As you now know, living a maximized life (one that reaches its full potential) is the byproduct of seeing yourself in the light of God's purpose for you. Your existence didn't take God by surprise because He placed you here to do something of value, something unique, something significant. You exist because the world needs what only you possess!

----------- ❖ -----------

Your Creator has pre-wired you for success.

When you find your reason for existence and begin to walk in that purpose, you will no longer be at the mercy of life's oncoming lawnmowers! No more will you see yourself as an ant-sized individual, but rather as the More Than Conqueror God created you to be.

My objective in this book has been to help you see yourself as God sees you. I want you to rejoice in the fact that you are the byproduct of a heavenly brainstorming session. At some moment in eternity past God said, "I want to see this purpose accomplished on earth." Then, at the appropriate time, He created you to *help* bring it to pass.

Grasshopper mentality doesn't stand a chance when we are committed to the above principles. However, there is one more truth, and when you embrace it, you will wipe away any final traces of that debilitating disease. This truth is to know that you are SPECIAL!

Coming to understand that you are "one of a kind" begins with the realization of where you came from. The word "special" means extraordinary, unique, and exceptional; and this is exactly what each of us is in God's sight. You and I are the pinnacle of His creation. Everything God created was good; but after He made us, He added an adverb to intensify the adjective which describes what He had made. He said it was "VERY good."[2]

What is it about us that makes us special? The answer is we were not patterned after monkeys, chimpanzees, or gorillas, but after Almighty God Himself. We find this truth in the first chapter of Genesis where we are told, "Then God said, 'Let us make people in our image, to be like ourselves.'"[3] This is what makes us special—a truth almost too wonderful to comprehend.

We often hear children talking about whom they wish they could grow up to be like. They will mention names such as, "When I grow up, I want to be like Michael Jordan," or "When I grow up I want to be like Tiger Woods." While these are good aspirations, they fall far short of the truth that you and I were created to be like God!

Scripture affirms this truth over and over, as in the eighth Psalm: "What is man that you are mindful of him and the son of man that you visit him? For you have made him a little lower than YOURSELF, and you have crowned him with glory and honor. You have made him to have dominion over the works of your hands; you have put all things under his feet."[4]

The Bible also encourages us to understand just how special we are when it tells us "we are gods and sons of the Most High."[5] These are astounding statements that speak to one amazing fact: we are special because we are like God!

The failure to realize this basic truth has left mankind throughout all ages feeling inferior and insignificant. From the beginning of time the enemy of our souls has tried to blind us to the fact that we are special because we are like God. After the Creator formed Adam and Eve and placed them in a paradise where good reigned over evil, Satan came along and caused the fall of both man and creation by challenging man's likeness to their Creator.

Now the serpent was more crafty than any of the wild animals the Lord God had made. He said to the woman, "Did God really say, 'You must not eat from any tree in the garden'?" The woman said to the serpent, "We may eat fruit from the trees in the garden, but God did say, 'You must not eat fruit from the tree that is in the middle of the garden, and you must not touch it, or you will die.'" "You will not surely die," the serpent said to the woman. For God knows that when you eat of it your eyes will be opened, and you will be like God, knowing good and evil." When the woman saw that the fruit of the tree was good for food and pleasing to the eye, and also desirable for gaining wisdom, she took some and ate it. She also gave some to her husband, who was with her, and he ate it.[6]

What a deception! Man was *already* like God. He didn't have to eat an apple to become God-like.

Sadly, we haven't learned our lesson. The enemy still has us convinced we are anything other than created in the image and likeness of God. The result has been nothing short of a devastating identity crisis which manifests itself in all sorts of self-effacing behavior. Many suicides and attempted suicides are due to man's unwarranted feeling of unimportance. Many mass murderers and serial killers confess there is a relationship between their destructive behavior and their need to feel important or superior.

The passion for relevance and significance even makes members of one race or ethnic group conceive reasons to think of themselves as superior to members of other groups and thereby it leads to prejudice which motivates inhumane behavior and social injustice. In like manner it also gives birth to tyrants and dictators who brutally violate the sanctity of human life and dignity for an unmerited sense of their own significance.

The desperate desire to feel important and relevant also

causes many individuals to abandon common sense, good judgment, moral standards, and basic human values, sometimes sacrificing excellent reputations and years of character-building lifestyles for the sake of advancement to a desired position or a place of recognition and fame in their society or workplace.

——————— ❖ ———————

*The search for significance and meaning
in life is the cause of and motivation for
all human behavior and conflict.*

It is a universal quest at all racial, ethnic, social, and economic strata. No one is immune.[7] The sad futility of it becomes evident when we come to understand that in the beginning God sought to give us the significance that we are searching for by making us and telling us we are like Him!

In keeping with this revelation, here are seven God-like characteristics all of us possess that make us S.P.E.C.I.A.L.

S—WE ARE SELF-WILLED

Have you ever wondered why the world sometimes seems to be spinning out of control? Sickness, disease, tsunamis, hurricanes, and wars are on the rise. It seems almost as if God has turned His back on us. And this may be the reason why many choose to ignore the Lord and refuse to place their faith in Him. But before falling into such an error, we need to take a closer look.

When God first created the world and man, He had nothing but good in mind. "The world He created was originally a wondrous place—a perfect environment suitable for every form of life. It was originally so perfect that there weren't even thorns or thistles. The soil produced bumper crops year every year. The earth was teeming with life—the skies full of birds and the waters brimming with fish. There were no predators, nor was there such a thing as death. Food was provided by lush vegetation that flourished unendangered by pollution. One could walk through the densest foliage without threat of dangerous animals, insects, or plants. Fear was an unknown word.

"The earth was truly the paradise God had meant it to be. No dangerous jungle. No over-soaked, deadly swamp. No barren desert. The earth was like what we now imagine *heaven* to be. Life was a pulsating, vibrant force. No sickness, no disease, no death. The world was a dynamic, aesthetically beautiful and tranquil place, made not by happenstance, but by design—a design in anticipation of His crowning creation. God designed the earth for you and me."[8]

And He created the earth as a Father who was about to establish a family. Scripture clearly tells us that God formed the heavens and the earth to be inhabited by His children.[9] "Man was not a spur-of-the-moment decision by God, nor was man an amazing coincidence of evolution. Man was the result of an elaborate, highly detailed plan purposely orchestrated by God,"[10] —the ultimate Father who went to great lengths to establish a perfect environment for His family.

The only missing element was love! So our Father set out to create a setting where true love could exist—a decision that carried with it a risk, because it involved giving man free will (or the ability to be self-willed), since choice is an essential requirement for true love.

As an illustration, try to imagine a marriage where every day, three times a day, the man asks his wife if she loves him and her response is always the same: "Yes, dear, I love you with all my heart." With this in mind, one might conclude that the marriage is founded on true love.

Let's add the detail, however, that the woman tells her husband that she loves him with all her heart only because he brutally beats her if she gives him any other answer. In other words, he uses his power to force her to do what he *wants* her to do.

Knowing this added fact, we can see that the above marriage is *not* based on true love. Instead, it is sustained only by conditioned responses prompted by fear.

———— ❖ ————

In order for true love to exist, there must be free will—the ability to choose regarding giving or withholding one's affection!

This illustration is revealing when we apply it to God's relationship with humanity. The Lord could have created us without the ability to choose to love, serve, and obey Him. He could have exercised His power over us to *force* us to submit to Him. But doing this would have countermanded the primary objective He had in mind—to create an environment of true love. So instead, He chose to give us the ability to choose, even though the provision carried with it the inevitable risk of adverse consequences resulting from bad choices.

Unfortunately, the gift of free will made it possible for our first ancestors to choose to disobey God and partake of the fruit of the Tree of Knowledge of Good and Evil—a choice with the direst of consequences: expulsion from paradise and the seemingly inevitable fate of death.

But God didn't entirely abandon us in His wrath, as the story above might seem to suggest. He did not leave us high and dry. Instead, the Creator did something quite special that we will describe in the next section. But for now we need only to understand it is self-will that makes us special, distinguishing us from the rest of His creation and making us like God. The Father loved us so much that He chose to keep His power in check by granting us the ability to choose or reject Him—this makes us more like God than does any other attribute He has built into us. It makes us a "very good" creation.

P—WE HAVE THE POWER TO DO GOOD

The second God-like attribute we have been given which makes us special is *power*. There is no need to elaborate on God's awesome power because the story of creation makes this quite obvious. But the power He has given to man needs further explanation.

Genesis tells us that as God contemplated His greatest creation, He said, *"Let us make man in our image, according to our likeness; let him have dominion [or power] over the fish of the sea, over the birds of the air, and over the cattle, over all the earth, and over every creeping thing that creeps on the earth."*[11]

It is clear, therefore, that God provided each of us with power—power we can use to hurt or to heal, to build or to destroy, to encourage or to disparage, to reach out to or to reject, to do good or to do evil. History is replete with tyrants like Hitler, Stalin, and Sadam Hussein, who chose to wield their power for dreadful purposes. But we are most like God when we use our strength and ability to do what is good.

Jesus knew this and admonished us with simple advice often referred to as The Golden Rule. He told us to ask ourselves what we want people to do for us, and then take the initiative to do it for them.[12] Many consider it the highpoint of the greatest sermon ever preached, The Sermon on the Mount—on how to relate to others.

Most of us have heard these words in various forms, and some have even come up with their revised versions of the message, such as "Do unto others *before* they do unto you," "Do unto others *after* they've done it to you," and "Do unto others one better than they have done unto you." And one little girl, confused as to the exact meaning of the famous rule, wrote a letter to God, asking Him for clarification. "Dear God," she wrote, "Did you really mean 'Do unto others *as* they do unto you? Because if You did, I'm really gonna fix my brother!'"

Whatever version of the Golden Rule you use, one thing is certain:

———— ❖ ————

What Jesus taught espouses a great truth—that you and I have the power to do good to others and that the beneficial use of this God-given power makes us very much like Him.

Many years ago, the desk clerk of a small Philadelphia hotel, after having told an elderly man and his wife that every guest room in the hotel had been taken, added, "But I can't send a nice couple like you out into the rain. Would you be willing to sleep in my room while I am here working?"

And with that the clerk gave the couple his room for the night. He had the power either to send them away or to perform an act of kindness. He chose the latter.

The next morning, the elderly man told the clerk, "You are the kind of person who should be the boss of the best hotel in the United States. Maybe someday I'll build it for you."

The clerk laughed and forgot about the incident. But two years later he received a letter containing a round trip ticket to New York and a request that he be the guest of the elderly couple.

After the clerk arrived in New York, the old man led him to the corner of Fifth Avenue and Thirty-fourth Street, where he pointed to a luxurious new building and declared, "This is the hotel I have just built for you to manage."

The young man, George C. Boldt, accepted the offer of William Waldorf Astor to become the manager of the original Waldorf Astoria Hotel.[13] The young clerk had made the choice to use his power to do good and learned it benefits not only the receiver of a good deed, also the doer.

Jesus chose to use *His* power for good. He could have remained with His Father and continued ruling the heavens and earth, but instead He used His power to come to earth and die on a cross for the sins of mankind. What you and I do with our power is up to us, but by putting our energies into doing what is honorable and right, we are following Jesus' example and are acting as *God* would act!

E—WE ARE EXCELLENT IN EVERY WAY

As we have noted, until He made man, God had called all His creations simply "good." But He described His creation of man as *"very* good," suggesting there was something extra special about man among all of His works. The New Living Translation of the Bible gives us a fresh insight when it tells us, *"God [then] looked over all he had made, and he saw that it was excellent in every way."*[14] This entitles man to a third special characteristic—that he too is *excellent in every way.*

Have you ever wondered why you are the way you are? Why you have the personality you have? Why you possess a particular assortment of gifts? Why you have certain likes and dislikes? Why you have physical and intellectual characteristics which distinguish you from others?

Most of us have wondered about these things; and sadly, many of us have done so with much remorse, wishing we were different instead of rejoicing in the person God created us to be.

This kind of thinking, however, only perpetuates grasshopper mentality. The Lord wants us to know we are uniquely formed for specific reasons. God designed you to accomplish the purpose He intended. This means you are perfect for your purpose—or *excellent in every way!* Even your "warts" and shortcomings are beautiful to God, as the popular Christmas fable about Rudolf the Red-Nosed Reindeer reminds us.

As the story goes, there were many days when Rudolf wished he were different. Especially since he had to endure the jokes and jeers of the rest of the reindeer, who refused to let him play in any of their games. Even Santa didn't consider Rudolf for a place on the reindeer team to pull his sleigh on Christmas Eve. And this was a crushing blow for Rudolf, since being chosen to help pull the Christmas sleigh was the dream of all the reindeer.

But one Christmas Eve a fierce snowstorm caused a whiteout that jeopardized the flight of Santa's sleigh and threatened the joy and excitement of all the little boys and girls who would wake up to find that Santa hadn't delivered any Christmas presents.

Fortunately, though, someone came up with the idea that Rudolf's shiny red nose could light the way! So Santa chose him to lead his reindeer team. Christmas was saved, and Rudolf no longer desired to be different, knowing there was a reason he had been blessed with his shiny red nose.

So the next time you think you don't fit in, remember Rudolf and realize that you are the way you are because God has a special plan for your life.

———— ❖ ————

The Creator designed you to be excellent in every way, even the parts you might like to change!

You never know whether the very thing you see as your greatest weakness may just be what God uses most.

C—WE HAVE CREATIVE POTENTIAL

Not only do our God-given attributes of self-will, power, and excellence make us special, but so does our creativity. Have you ever found yourself amazed by the genius of mankind? Thomas Edison invented the phonograph and the incandescent light bulb,

Alexander Graham Bell invented the telephone. German scientist Karl Braun invented the cathode ray tube that serves as the picture tube found in modern TV sets. Wilbur and Orville Wright pioneered the powered airplane, which they patented as a "flying machine." Henry Ford conceived and introduced the Model T automobile that heralded the beginning of the Motor Age. The list of man's creative achievements is endless!

Of course, no real quantitative parallel can be drawn between man's inventive potential and the limitless creative power of God so impressively chronicled in the book of Genesis. Nevertheless, man's God-given abilities are undeniable.

———— ❖ ————

Unlimited potential resides in each of us from before the time we can even walk or talk.

One of my good friends has a young son, Wesley, whose obvious affection for me probably has something to do with the bucket of tokens I gave him to play the games in our church arcade, where he rode in one of our toy cars. We put a token in the slot and off he went, with the car rocking and jerking to music.

Later, Wesley amazed me by making a tiny replica of the toy car for me out of tape and paper—an astonishing creative accomplishment quite illustrative of one of many ways in which God has made us like Him.

And our creative ability makes us feel good. The smile of achievement on Wesley's face when he handed me his miniature masterpiece reminded me of the same look of satisfaction I used to see on my father's face after he had finished cutting the lawn, painting a room or rebuilding his 1978 Ford Pinto. And why not? Such feelings of accomplishment are not unlike, in their own way, the pleasure God, the source of our own creative genius, must have felt when He looked over all He had created and pronounced it "very good."[15]

So the next time you're tempted to relapse into grasshopper mentality, reflect on your creative achievements—the meal you just made for your family, the room design you just laid out, the strategic plan you spearheaded at work, or even the outfit you pulled together for that party last week. The sense of pride you feel from such accomplishments is a reminder of one significant way God has made you SPECIAL.

I—WE HAVE THE POWER TO IMAGINE

Our creative potential is often activated by the fifth characteristic God has built into each one of us to make us special—our imagination. Unfortunately, organized religion has frowned upon this wonderful gift for so long that many people of faith have suppressed their imagination. Having been led to believe that using our thoughts may stray and lead to the pursuit of carnal pleasures, many have turned their backs on this God-given gift.

But what if the Lord had never given Himself over to imagining? The answer is that you and I would have never been born. Yes, purpose was the original intent in the mind of God (our Creator) which motivated Him to create us. But it was God's imagination that gave form to His creation.

———— ❖ ————

In order to create we must first formulate the design within our mind's eye—because imagination always precedes creation.

The story behind Walt Disney World in Florida reminds us of this truth. Mr. Disney died before the Grand Opening, so his wife was asked to appear on the stage at the ribbon cutting in his stead. When she was introduced, the master of ceremonies said, "Mrs. Disney, I only wish that Walt could have seen this."

Mrs. Disney's quick response was "He did!"[16] Walt Disney had vividly conceived the design of the theme park in his imagination, and his vision spawned its creation.

Our creative mind is not unlike the "transporter" in the television Star Trek episodes that Captain Kirk was thinking of when he clicked open his communicator and commanded, "Beam me up, Scotty."

Scotty would then activate the "transporter," which would "beam up" any member of the Enterprise crew from anywhere in the universe back to the mother ship. The device worked by de-materializing people or things in one place and instantaneously re-materializing them in another.

Our imagination is like that transporter. This God-given faculty, when operated properly and in accordance with the Creator's instructions, brings the invisible things seen only in our mind's eye into the material world. In other words, it materializes our dreams.

Emerson described this process when he said, "Sow a thought, reap an action." Our minds were made to figure out ways to do what they are imagining. When we set about visualizing, our brain shifts gears to the creative mode and begins to give us ideas concerning how to accomplish what we are imagining. First comes thought, then the organization of the vision into reality.

So if anyone tries to thwart your gift of imagination, remember that all things are always created twice—first in our mind, then for the world to see.

This amazing power to inspire our God-like creativity is illustrated by an event in the life of one of the world's greatest artists, Michelangelo. In 1463, when members of the City Council of Florence, Italy, decided they needed a monument to grace their city, they commissioned a sculptor to carve a giant statue to stand in front of their City Hall. Someone suggested a biblical character as the subject—wrought in the neoclassical style as an expression of beauty and strength.

They approached Agostino di Duccio, who, having agreed to their terms, went to the quarry near Carrara and marked off a nineteen-foot slab to be cut from the white marble. He had the slab cut too thin, however; and when the block was removed, it fell, leaving a deep fracture down one side. The sculptor declared the stone useless and demanded another, but the city council refused. Consequently, the gleaming block of marble lay on its side for the next thirty-eight years as a visible public embarrassment.

Then, in 1501, the council approached another citizen, the son of a local official, and asked him if he would complete the ambitious project, using the broken slab. Fortunately for them, the young man was Michelangelo Buonarroti, a twenty-six-year-old artist who was richly endowed with both skill and *imagination*.

Michelangelo locked himself in a workshop behind the cathedral and chiseled and polished away on the stone for three years. And when the work was finished, it took forty-nine men five days to carry it to the City Hall. Archways were torn down and narrow streets were widened so the expression of a young man's imagination could be properly placed and displayed.

Afterwards, people from across Europe came to see the fourteen-foot statue of David relaxing after defeating Goliath. It was even more than the city fathers had envisioned. The giant stone had been transformed from the massive fractured waste of rock into a masterpiece surpassing the art of either Greece or Rome[17]—all because of a young man who was willing to use his imagination to give wings to his God-like talent.

A—WE HAVE THE POWER TO OFFER OTHERS THE GIFT OF ACCEPTANCE

Acceptance means you see yourself as valuable just as you are. It allows you to be the real you. You are not tempted to accept anyone else's idea of who you are. It means you respect your own ideas because you respect *yourself*—and you can talk about how you feel inside and why you feel that way unselfconsciously and without fear of rejection.

Thankfully, acceptance leads to self-assurance. However, this doesn't mean you will never be shown to be wrong or that you should refuse to accept criticism; but it indicates you will feel safe expressing yourself freely.

———————— ❖ ————————

In short, acceptance simply makes you feel free to be yourself, even if others don't approve of what you say or do. You respect yourself as you are.

God allowed Adam and Eve to enjoy this gift even after they had sinned. In the third chapter of Genesis we are told that after exercising their self-will and choosing to disobey God, the Lord called out to them in the garden. And when they heard His voice, they hid themselves from His presence, knowing full well they had disobeyed.

Aware they had lost their innocence and therefore ashamed of being without clothes, God asked them rhetorically why they were hiding, and they replied, "Because we are naked."

The Creator then expressed His displeasure over their decision to sin and told them of the consequences which would ensue. But in His compassionate understanding of the distress they were feeling because of their newly acquired knowledge of good and evil, He covered their nakedness with animal skins and offered them the gift of acceptance. He didn't condone their sin, nor did He exempt them from its consequences; but He loved them as they were. And His gift of acceptance made possible their eventual redemption and reconciliation[18]

Jesus also offered this same gift to many with whom He came in contact as He walked the earth. One such instance is found in Luke, chapter seven. The setting was an aristocratic dinner party in the home of Simon, one of the leading Pharisees. Simon had decided to invite Jesus to his home for dinner, along with many of the movers and shakers of Jesus' time; and contrary to popular expectation, Jesus accepted the invitation.

All the preparations had been carefully planned and executed. A doorman had been stationed at the entrance to ensure only those on the "A" list were allowed in.

The dinner party was going just perfectly, with everyone partaking of the elaborate hors d'oeuvres, when all of a sudden an uninvited but well-known "guest" appeared on the scene—well-known not because of her contributions to society, but because of her scorned behavior as the town prostitute.

If interrupting the elite dinner party were not shameful enough, the infamous woman pushed past the doorman, made a beeline for Jesus, and began wailing at His feet.

Everyone was silent but obviously appalled—everyone, that is, except Jesus. And if her actions hadn't shocked the guests, what she did next certainly did. She took an alabaster box of very expensive perfume and began to anoint Jesus' body with its ointment while washing his feet with her tears. This prompted jeers and brow-lifting expressions of disgust, surprisingly not directed at the woman of ill repute, but at Jesus Himself.

The choice confronting Jesus was obvious: either to reject her because of her sin and gain the favor of the dinner guests or to accept her and be ridiculed.

Jesus chose the latter course, offering the undeserving woman the gift of acceptance.

He chose this response because, like God the Father, He saw people differently than you and I often view them. We tend to judge others externally, while God sees past our tattered exteriors to the potential which resides inside.

Let me share this pertinent story. On a bright, hot summer day on a windswept Caribbean island, an old sculptor made his way to his humble home outside the village center. On his way, he passed by the great white mansion of the plantation owner who, with his field workers, was felling one of the ancient trees that had provided protection from the scorching sun for generations.

The old sculptor suddenly stopped and, with an interested twinkle in his eyes, called over the wall, "What will you do with those discarded stumps of wood?"

"They are good for nothing but firewood," the owner replied. "I have no use for this junk."

The sculptor begged for a piece of the "junk" wood, carefully lifted the knotted tree trunk onto his shoulders, and, smiling gratefully, staggered into the distance with his burdensome treasure.

Arriving at his cottage, the old man placed the jagged piece of tree in the center of the floor and ceremoniously walked around what the plantation owner had called "useless junk." Then, with a strange smile on his leathered face, the elderly gentleman picked up his hammer and chisel and attacked the wood, working as if under a mandate to set something free from the gnarled, weathered trunk.

The following morning's sun found the sculptor asleep on his cottage floor, clutching a beautifully sculptured bird that he had freed from the bondage of the discarded wood. And when he awoke, he set the bird on the railing of his front porch and forgot it.

Weeks later, when the plantation owner was passing by and saw the bird, he asked to buy it, offering whatever price the sculptor might name. Then, satisfied he had made an excellent bargain, he walked away, hugging his newly acquired treasure with great pride.

The old sculptor counted his spoil and thought to himself, "Junk or beauty is in the eyes of the beholder. Some look, but others see."[19]

All around us are people who, like that old tree, have been rejected or discarded for one reason or another. But they should never either discredit themselves or accept the rebuff of others. All they need is someone to offer them the gift of acceptance and, by so doing, help them to release the potential God has given them.

Just as the old sculptor saw something in the wood that no one else could see and undertook to liberate it,

---------- ❖ ----------

Jesus saw something in the prostitute the other guests couldn't see—God's investment of potential within her—and offered her the gift of acceptance to help her set it free.

Perhaps you, like the old sculptor and Jesus, are the vehicle God wants to use to release the beauty hidden deep within someone that He sees as special!

L—WE HAVE THE POWER TO LOVE THE UNLOVABLE

The last of the seven God-like characteristics that make us special, but certainly not the least, is the power we possess to love the undeserved. As we will see, this is possibly our greatest God-like attribute; but it is also the one most foreign to us. We live in a world where love is either deserved or earned, and where any expression of love which falls outside these parameters is subject to suspicion or rejection.

There is, however, a system of love that operates on a higher level—God's system, which is succinctly described in one very powerful scripture: "Love your enemies! Do good to them! Lend to them! And don't be concerned that they might not repay. Then your reward from heaven will be very great, and you will truly be acting as children of the Most High, for he is kind to the unthankful and to those who are wicked."[20]

Notice that God's system of love is quite different from ours, since it is in no way based on apparent merit. He operates on the Agape Love system.

Agape is one of the Greek words for love used in the New Testament. It stands in stark contrast to our earned system of love because it has to do with the mind. Rather than love based on a payback or an emotion that simply rises unbidden in our hearts, it is a principle by which we deliberately love. It essentially has to do with our will. It is a conquest, a victory, and an achievement.

No one ever naturally loves his enemies since this requires control over or denial of all our natural inclinations and emotions. The Agape system is a deliberate principle of the mind and supreme expression of our first God-like attribute—our self will. Agape is in fact the power to love the unlovable and undeserving.

Notice that in the Scripture quoted above we are told when we love like this, we are acting like God. The passage goes on to illustrate the Father's unconditional love by stating *"he sends his rain on the just and the unjust and on the evil and the good."* In short, no matter what an individual is like, whether he be a saint or a sinner, God seeks nothing but his highest good.

This is what *agape* teaches us. It is the spirit that tells us no matter what any man does to us, we will never seek to harm him or set out for revenge. We will always pursue nothing but his highest good.

———— ❖ ————

God's love is unconquerable benevolence and invincible good will.

It is not simply a wave of emotion or an act motivated by an expectation of repayment. It is a deliberate achievement, conquest and victory of the will. It takes all of us to achieve this.[21]

The most telling attribute of heavenly love, however, is its power to change people for the better, as illustrated in the story of Norma McCorvey, better known to most of us as the Jane Roe in the Supreme Court's 1973 Roe v. Wade decision.

Quite a while after this landmark ruling, and to the shock of many, Norma was baptized by Flip Benham, National Director of Operation Rescue. The events leading to her baptism started with an apology. Early in 1995, Benham had relocated the organization's national headquarters to a building next to the abortion clinic where McCorvey worked. And that same week Benham spoke to McCorvey, apologizing for an earlier encounter, when he had told her she was responsible for millions of abortions. "I saw that those words really hurt you," he told her, and asked for her forgiveness.

Though she admitted Benham's comment had really caused her pain, she accepted his apology, and the two struck up a friendship.

Even before her conversion, McCorvey spoke freely about the friendship. "I like Flip," McCorvey told a reporter. "He's doing his thing." And the unconditional love that Benham and other Operation Rescue workers showed McCorvey eventually broke through.

Although she was an icon of the pro-abortion movement, McCorvey had felt used. But as she saw firsthand the love of Christ through her new friends, she eventually felt more comfortable with them than she did with her clinic coworkers. She even dropped by OR's offices and sometimes answered the phone for them when no one else was available. This love and acceptance led McCorvey to a Dallas area church, where in late July of 1995 she put her life into God's hands. "Jane Roe was the person whom the pro-abortion side cared about most,"

Benham commented, "but God was always concerned with Norma McCorvey."

This non-condemning love continues. McCorvey quit her job at the clinic and accepted employment with Operation Rescue. She and Benham, however, still don't see eye-to-eye on every issue. "We've got to give her some time and space," says Benham. "Changes on such a personal level take a little bit longer."[22]

McCorvey's conversion reminds all of us of the mighty force of unconditional love to change people for the better. You and I also have this power, and it makes us special.

—————— ❖ ——————

These seven simple God-like, God-given characteristics remind us that we are extraordinary in His sight.

We are self willed, have the power to do good, are excellent in every way, possess creative ability, have the power to imagine, to offer others the gift of acceptance, and a heart to love the unlovable.

These all point to one fabulous truth—that none of us is a grasshopper—as Mikhael for so long tragically imagined himself to be. We have a new identity. We are like God!

A PERSONAL MESSAGE FROM THE AUTHOR

THE FINAL CURE FOR GRASSHOPPER MENTALITY

O n the subject of how to overcome grasshopper mentality, one theme has continually surfaced: Discovering Your Purpose.

Purpose, as we now know, is the original intent in our Creator's mind which motivated Him to breath life into us. So in order for us to discover this, we must somehow gain access to God, because only He can reveal our purpose to us. But how do you and I gain entrance into the presence of God?

Jesus Christ Himself answered this question for us in the Gospel of Saint John: "I am the way, the truth, and the life. No one comes to the Father except through me."

Each of us is a sinner at heart, and every one of us has sinned against God.[1] And this both separates us from Him and imposes the penalty of eternal separation from our Creator in a place called Hell.[2]

Of course, you or I might try to make restitution for our sin in order to reconcile ourselves with God. But how can we accomplish this? And what is the penalty for each individual sin?

For example, suppose that as you were commuting to work,

someone were to cut you off and you began shouting in anger and motioning obscenely at the offending driver.

How might you (or I) pay for a sin of this nature? What is the penalty for such a trespass? The price of gasoline is easy to determine, as is the cost of a gallon of milk or a loaf of bread. But what is the price we pay for becoming angry with an aggressive driver during a rush-hour commute? Do you wave and smile benignly at the next ten drivers you see? To how many drivers do you have to be courteous to make restitution for your sin? Twenty? Fifty?

The answer is that no one can be sure of the exact price to be paid to compensate for a given sin. But one thing is certain: there is a debt to pay, and, as Romans 6:23 tells us, it is eternal separation from God in a place called Hell.

There are only two possible ways to pay the debt imposed on us for iniquity. We can either pay the cost or find someone else to pay it for us.

But who would agree to assume our debt and pay the price for our sins? Who would willfully separate himself from God and sentence himself to Hell?

There is a remarkable facility near the city of São Josédos Campos, Brazil, where several decades ago the Brazilian government turned a prison over to two Christians who renamed it "Humaita" with the idea of running it on biblical principles. There are only two full-time staff members, and all of the work is done by inmates. And families outside the prison walls adopt inmates to work with during and after their terms of imprisonment.

After visiting the prison, Chuck Colson reported that he found the inmates smiling—particularly the murderer who held the keys, opened the gates, and let him in. Wherever he walked he saw men at peace, cleaning living areas and working industriously. The walls were decorated with sayings from Psalms and Proverbs. His guide escorted him to the notorious prison cell once used for torture. Today, the inmate told him, that block housed only a single prisoner. Then, as they reached the end of a long concrete corridor and the guard put the key into the lock, he paused and asked Colson, "Are you sure you want to go in?"

"Of course," Colson replied impatiently. "I've been in isolation cells all over the world."

The guard swung open the massive door, and Colson saw the "prisoner" in the punishment cell: a crucifix, beautifully carved by the Humaita inmates, with the "prisoner"Jesus hanging on a cross.

"He's doing time for the rest of us," Colson's guide told him softly.[3]

It sometimes takes those whose sin has caused them to pay a social price to make us see the eternal price of our transgressions.

———— ❖ ————

You can either try to pay the penalty for your sin on your own and be left wondering whether you have really cancelled your debt, or you can accept what Jesus Christ has done in our place and be sure to be reconciled with God.

The choice is yours, but the stakes are high. I believe the only certain decision is to accept Christ's payment for our sin. When we do, we are guaranteed access to God, thereby enabling us to discover our divinely intended purpose and to receive eternal life.

If you choose to give your life to Jesus Christ today and receive Him as your personal Lord and Savior, just pray this prayer from your heart:

Heavenly Father, today I give my heart completely and wholly to You. I recognize I am a sinner and that I need a Savior. Therefore I invite Jesus Christ to be the Lord of my life. I accept and put my faith in His finished work on Calvary's Cross as payment in full for my sins.

Thank you, Jesus, for the price you paid on the cross and the victory You won in Your resurrection from the dead. And thank you, Father, for receiving me as Your child. From this day forward I vow to glorify You with my life as You reveal to me my purpose for living.

In Jesus' name I pray, Amen!

REFERENCES

Unless otherwise noted, all Scripture references are taken from the Holy Bible, New King James Version.

CHAPTER ONE

1. Numbers 13:31-33.2
2 Corinthians 6:7
3. Numbers 13:33
4. 1 Samuel 15:17 (NIV)
5. 1 Peter 1:18-19
6. Romans 5:8 (NIV)
7. Exodus 4:14
8. Romans 8:37
9. *Ibid.*, 8:28
10. John 10:10
11. Morris, Van. Source: Helen Keller, *The Story of MyLife* (Doubleday, 1954).[www.preachingtoday.com]
12. 1 Corinthians 15:33 NAS
13. 1 Kings 17:1-16
14. Hebrews 12:2
15. John 12:32
16. [www.bible.org/illus.asp?topic id=442]
17. *Ibid.*, id=213
18. 2 Kings 6:15-17
19. Matthew 23:11
20. 1 Corinthians 3:14
21. Isaiah 43:25
22. *Ibid.*, 59:19
23. Ecclesiastes 9:11
24. Jobs, Steve. 2005 commencement address at Stanford University. Submitted by Greg Asimakoupoulous. [www.preachingtoday.com]

CHAPTER TWO

1. Numbers 13:33
2. 2 Corinthians 10:3-5
3. Proverbs 23:7
4. *Theology News and Notes*, October 1976, quoted in Multnomah Message, Spring1993, p. 1. [www.bible.org/illus.asp? topic_id =721]
5. 2 Corinthians 2:11 KJV
6. Rick Renner, *Spiritual Weapons to Defeat the Enemy* (Tulsa: Albury Publishing, 1992), p. 13
7. Philippians 4:13
8. Mark 10:27
9. 2 Corinthians 2:14
10. Romans 12:2
11. Commentary about the film *The Piano* (Miramax Films, 1993). Submitted by Greg Asimakoupoulousand Doug Scott. [preachingtoday.com]
12. Philippians 3:13
13. 2 Corinthians 7:2
14. *Ibid.*, 5:17
15. Numbers 14:2-3
16. *Idem*
17. 2 Corinthians 4:8-9
18. Deuteronomy 1:2-3
19. *Ibid.*, 1:6
20. John 5:2-7
21. Numbers 13:30
22. James 2:26
23. Deuteronomy 8:3-4
24. Psalm 119:130
25. Deuteronomy 11:24-25
26. James 1:17

CHAPTER THREE

1. Romans 8:37
2. Matthew 25:21
3. Genesis 12:2

4. Johnston, Jon. *You Can Stand Strong in the Face of Fear*, 1990, SP Publications, pp. 56-58. [bible.org/illus.asp?topic_id=334]

5. James 1:17

6. Myles Munroe, In Pursuit of Purpose (Shippensburg, PA: Destiny Image Publishers, 1992), p. 6

7. 1 Samuel 17:51

8. Jeremiah 29:11

9. Piper, Watty. From "The Little Engine that Could"(New York: Platt and Monl Publishing, 1976). [www.members.tripod.com/ ah_coo/engine_that_could.htm]

10. Joshua 1:8

11. 1 John 3:8

12. John 11:43

13. Luke 4:36

14. John 18:37

15. Exodus 3:10

16. *Ibid.*, 4:10

17. *Ibid.*, 4:11-12

18. *Ibid.*, 4:13

19. *Ibid.*, 4:14-15

20. *Ibid.*, 4:6

21. *Ibid.*, 5:1

22. Ephesians 2:20 NLT

23. Psalm 139:14

24. Joel Osteen, *Your Best Life Now* (New York, NY:Warner Faith, 2004)

25. Psalms 139:14

26. David J. Schwartz, Ph. D., *The Magic of Thinking Big* (New York, NY: Simon & Schuster, 1987)

27. Exodus 4:10

28. Romans 12:2

29. Myles Munroe, In Pursuit of Purpose (Shippensburg, PA: Destiny Image Publishers, 1992), p. 6

30. Psalms 127:4

31. 1 Samuel 17:28-29

32. *Ibid.*, 17:33

33. *Ibid.*, 17:34-37

34. *Ibid.*, 17:43-44

35. *Ibid.*, 17:45-47

36. Crites, Dr. Paul. *Discovering the Power of Purpose* (Clearwater, Florida: Wonbyone Concepts, 1999),pp. 17-19

CHAPTER FOUR

1. Myles Munroe, *In Pursuit of Purpose* (Shippensburg, PA: Destiny Image Publishers, 1992), pp. 1-3

2. Proverbs 10:22

3. Luke 9:25

4. Munroe, p. 141

5. *Ibid.*, pp. 141-142

6. *Ibid.*, p. 142-143

7. Jeremiah 1:5

8. Pentz, Victor. From the sermon "The Gourmet God," delivered at Peachtree Presbyterian Church, Atlanta, Georgia (11/23/03). [www.preachingtoday.com]

9. 1 Timothy 6:17

10. Psalms 37:4

11. John 16:24

12. Campolo, Tony. "If I Should Wake before I Die,"Preaching Today, Tape No. 124. [www.preachigtoday.com]

13. Matthew 21:12-13

14. *U.S. News and World Report*, June 14, 1993, p. 37

15. John 11:35-44

16. Christianity Today International. "The Southeast Outlook," 12/16/04. Submitted by Van Morris. [www.preachingtoday.com].

17. Munroe, p. 45

18. 2 Corinthians 10:12

19. Romans 12:6-8

20. 2 Timothy 4:7 and Philippians 3:10

21. Proverbs 4:7-9

22. 2 Chronicles 1:7-11

CHAPTER FIVE

1. Philippians 3:12-14 NIV

2. James 2:20

3. Proverbs 24:16

4. Galatians 6:9

5. *Bits and Pieces*, August 20, 1992, pp. 16-18. www.bible.org/illus. asp?topic_id=1219]

6. 1 Samuel 17:25-27

7. About the film *Cinderella Man*, Universal Studios,2005. Submitted by Bill While, Paramount, California. [www.preachingtoday.com]

8. Ecclesiastes 1:2 NIV

9. Myles Munroe, *In Pursuit of Purpose* (Shippensburg, PA: Destiny Image Publishers, 1992), introduction

10. *Bits and Piece*, November 1989, p. 12

11. Munroe, introduction

12. [http://yourquotations.net/Booker%20T%Washington quotes.html]

13. Dr. Paul Crites, *Discovering the Power of Purpose* (Clearwater, Florida: Wonbyone Concepts, 1999), pp. 36-37

14. Psalms 139:14

15. Luke 5:4

16. John 5:6

17. Mark 12:43

18. Matthew 8:10

19. Matthew 4:19

20. Luke 19:5

21. Mark 5:34

22. John 11:43

23. Matthew 14:16

24. Matthew 26:7-10

25. Luke 24:49

26. John 8:3-8

27. Psalms 91:1,9-11,16

28. Isaiah 54:17

29. Luke 8:22-25

30. Philippians 2:13

31. Exodus 3:10

CHAPTER SIX

1. 2 Corinthians 10:4-5
2. University of Chicago study
3. Matthew 25:21
4. 2 Timothy 4:7
5. Proverbs 13:12
6. Submitted by Eric Hulstrand, Binford, North Dakota. [http://elbourne.org/ sermons/index.mv?illustration+4964]
7. Genesis 8:22
8. Galatians 6:7
9. Ecclesiastes 11:1
10. Proverbs 28:19 NIV
11. Burford, Sherman L. In *Fresh Illustrations for Preaching and Teaching* (Baker), from the editorsof *Leadership*. [www.preachingtoday,com]
12. Dr. Paul Crites, *Discovering the Power of Purpose* (Clearwater, Florida: Wonbyone Concepts, 1999), pp. 21-22
13. Submitted by Jason Cruise. [www.preachingtoday.com]
14. Joshua 1:1
15. 2 Timothy 2:2
16. Crites, p. 62-63
17. *Ibid.,* 63-64
18. Lee, Victor. "Sports Spectrum," reprinted in *Men of Integrity*. [www.preachingtoday.com]
19. Ephesians 6:8
20. John Hagee, "Joseph's Journey: The Pit to the Palace"tape series (San Antonio, TX: John Hagee Ministreis)
21. Genesis 1:26
22. Proverbs 4:18

CHAPTER SEVEN

1. Genesis 1:26
2. Hebrews 11:6
3. 2 Timothy 1:7
4. Romans 12:3
5. Genesis 1:26
6. Ibid, 11:6

7. Acts 2:1-4

8. Mark 9:23

9. Dew, Diane. "Faith of a Little Child." [www.dianedew.com/grntrike.htm]

10. Myles Munroe, *In Pursuit of Purpose* (Shippensburg, PA: Destiny Image Publishers, 1992), p. 60

11. Myles Munroe, *Maximizing Your Potential* (Shippensburg, PA: Destiny Image Publishers, 1996), p.5.

12. Proverbs 29:25

13. Munroe, p. 5

14. *Ibid.*, preface

15. *Ibid.*, p. 6

16. *Ibid.*, preface

17. 2 Timothy 4:6-7

18. Munroe, p. 4

19. Isaiah 53:12

20. Munroe, p. 1-2

21. *Ibid.*, p. 12

22. *Ibid.*, p. 8

23. *Ibid.*, p. 6-8

24. *Ibid.*, p. 9

25. 2 Corinthians 10:12-13

26. Munroe, pp. 6-7.

CHAPTER EIGHT

1. Romans 8:37

2. Genesis 1:31

3. Genesis 1:26 NLT

4. Psalms 8:4-6

5. Psalms 82:6

6. Genesis 3:1-6 NIV

7. Myles Munroe, *In Pursuit of Purpose* (Shippensburg, PA: Destiny Image Publishers, 1996), preface

8. Gregg Wear, *Beating the Blame Game* (Sedalia, MO: Gregg Wear, 1999), pp. 23-24

9. Psalms 115:6 and Isaiah 45:18

10. Wear, p. 28

11. Genesis 1:26

12. Matthew 7:12 Msg

13. From "Our Daily Bread." [www.bible.org]

14. Genesis 1:31 NLT

15. Ibid, NKJV

16. Myles Munroe, *The Principles and Power of Vision* (New Kensington, PA: Whitaker House, 2003), p.18

17. Whatley, Sam. *Pondering the Journey* (True Life Publishers, 2002), pp. 17-18. Submitted by David Long, Montgomery, Alabama. [www.preachingtoday.com]

18. Genesis 3

19. Myles Munroe, Understanding Your Potential (Shippensburg, PA: Destiny Image Publishers,2002), pp. 19-20

20. Luke 6:35 NLT

21. William Barclay, *New Testament Words* (Louisville, KY: Westminster John Knox Press, 1974), pp. 21-22

22. *Christian America*, October 1995, p 4. [www.bible,org/illus.asp?topic_id=756].

A PERSONAL MESSAGE FROM THE AUTHOR

1. Romans 3:23

2. Romans 6:23

3. Max Lucado, *In the Grip of Grace* (Dallas, TX: Word Publishing, 1996), p. 113

FOR A COMPLETE LIST OF MEDIA RESOURCES OR TO SCHEDULE THE AUTHOR FOR SPEAKING ENGAGEMENTS, CONTACT:

FRANK SANTORA
FAITH CHURCH
600 DANBURY ROAD
NEW MILFORD, CT 06776

PHONE: 860-354-7700
INTERNET: www.faithchurchct.com